MY JESUS

DAVID JOHNSON ROWE

On the cover: David Moss' composite images of Jesus broaden and deepen our appreciation of Jesus' universality. At the top is a painting by El Greco, *Savior*. To the right is a sixth century mosaic. To the left is *Navajo Compassionate Christ* by Father John Giuliani (1932-2021). Special gratitude to the friends and colleagues of Father John for permission. These representations and others equally thought-provoking may be found in *The Face of Jesus* (Edward Lucie-Smith, Abrams NY 2011).

Copyright © 2021 by David Johnson Rowe
All rights reserved. This book or any portion thereof may not be reproduced or used in any manner without the permission of the author.
Contact information: DRowe@greenfieldhillchurch.com
ISBN 978-1-257-09578-0

Proceeds from this book are given to the work of FOCI (Friends of Christ in India). For more information, visit the website at www.foci.org.

Dedication

To all my family
near and far
young and old
DNA shared or borrowed
each and every one
trying to do what Jesus would do
in surprising ways

Table of Contents

1. Are We Bored Yet? The Jesus Quest 1
2. My Journey With Jesus 16
3. Jesus in the Bible 38
4. Jesus' Kerygma 63
5. Jesus Teaches Me a Thing or Two 76
6. Jesus Doesn't Want Me For a Sunbeam 88
7. Lists of Kerygma 107
8. God as Opera 121
9. What If I'm Wrong? 140
10. The End 156

Acknowledgments

Alida Ward, my co-pastor and my wife, whose connection with Jesus is earth-bound and heaven-sent, and whose editing is always spot-on.

Camaron Rowe Vallepalli, whose keen eye and wise corrections greatly improved the final manuscript.

Tomáš Halík, whose friendship and mentorship have been a career-shaping inspiration and whose courage and wisdom lift my sights every day.

Carolyn Houghton, whose care of the manuscript made short work of long pages, accomplished with speed and grace.

David Moss, whose cover montage moves us toward the universal Jesus.

Greenfield Hill Congregational Church, whose embrace of "Christlikeness" makes every day an honor to serve.

Roni Widmer, whose ability to keep church life in order and serene is a blessing.

The friends of Father John Giuliani, whose *Navajo Compassionate Christ* graces the cover. Father John's legacy of expanding our understanding of Jesus through art is highlighted on the website and gallery established to share his work: JBGicon.com.

And my readers, whose engagement with words and ideas and faith make writing a worthwhile journey.

It is Christ Himself, not the Bible, who is the true Word of God. The Bible, read in the right spirit and with the guidance of good teachers, will bring us to Him. We must not use the Bible as a sort of encyclopedia out of which texts can be taken for use as a weapon.

- C.S. Lewis

One

Are We Bored Yet? The Jesus Quest

I was told that the beauty of a memoir is that you don't have to worry about accuracy. It's a memoir, after all, your memory of whatever. Put "my" in front of a title and it doesn't have to be proof checked.

A friend said he liked me because I always spoke the truth. Granted, he said, it might be a different truth from what I said yesterday or might say tomorrow, but in the moment he could count on me to speak the truth as I knew it. It was high praise, but a low bar.

I've used the possessive "my" before in several books and essays. I told my stories, my views, and my beliefs, while striving always to get it all correct.

Does the "My" in front of "Jesus" make this task simpler? Does it cut me some slack? Or is the very topic of Jesus so momentous that I had better be sure, not just truthful for today? Right, not just opinionated.

Yes.

What I offer is personal, experiential, and faithful. Yet, in the language of my grandfather Linwood, one day I will stand before the throne of God, the King of Kings and Lord of Lords, and will need to answer for all my thoughts, deeds and words. And words. These words. My words.

Though this book reflects on "My Jesus," reading and reflecting upon the Jesus of others has been an essential part of my own journey. From the Jesus of first century Gospel writers, second century church communities, third century church fathers, fourth century creeds, to the Jesus of medieval art, 18th century French philosophers, and 20th century German theologians; from the heroes of my personal faith journey to the giants of New England and American Protestantism, I have taken into account the myriad depictions of Jesus.

And there are plenty. Richard Wightman Fox, in *Jesus in America*, walks us through some of the uniquely American expressions of Jesus. There were the Pilgrims and Puritans with their fierce independence matched by strict structure and dogma. America had the exuberances of awakenings and revivals and Pentecostalism, moving from the orderly progression of faith to the anxieties of awaiting Jesus' return. We contemplated a "God is Dead" or "God is Irrelevant" mindset, while urging a personal relationship with Christ. Jesus remains a dominant presence in American history.

If you want to walk a lot deeper in the weeds, Charlotte Allen's *The Human Christ* takes you there, and you may not get out. Her tour de force covers three hundred years of what Albert Schweitzer popularly called "The Quest for the Historical Jesus." At the risk of audaciously oversimplifying Allen's work, my summation of it is that World Christianity has gone from "The Church declares. Period" to "The Bible says it, I believe it, that settles it" to "Who knows what's true in the Bible, anyway?!" Far more elegantly, Allen's book shows each generation making their own gigantic leaps of faith in order to strip away what they think is not authentic to

Jesus of Nazareth himself. This ranges from Thomas Jefferson literally taking scissors to the Four Gospels to cut away anything that did not meet his Deistic, rationalist standard to the late 20th Century Jesus Seminar which voted each year on which "red letter" verses of Jesus are red enough to be real Jesus.

More to the point, we are shown scholars and churches and individual Christians trying to understand the origins of scripture, and therefore the veracity of Jesus. Historical Criticism, Redaction Criticism, Literary Form and Text Criticism, demythologizing, even psychoanalyzing are tools used to get at who Jesus was, what he meant, and how he relates to today. In other words, who got to tell Jesus' story, how did they know it, and what are we to make of it?

In not so short order, our familiar friendly Jesus of Sunday School is presented to us as a romantic universalist, mythologized moralist, apocalypse-obsessed madman, a wandering Cynic sage, ardent feminist, failed political revolutionary, upsetter of apple carts, magician, cult leader, hallucinogenic, Shaman, a Divine idiot savant, a pan-Mediterranean carpenter, a simple Rabbi, and early Gary Cooper. Forgive me if I skipped one or two.

With my head spinning, yet intrigued, I was reminded of the old story of a scholar whose theory was that none of the works attributed to William Shakespeare were written by William Shakespeare, but instead were written by another Englishman named William Shakespeare.

My Jesus

At some point we are left with faith, which the Bible marvelously defines as "the substance of things hoped for, the evidence of things not seen" (Hebrews 11:1).

In other words, I know what I know. Jesus matters.

Thank goodness, I stumbled across the writings of Jaroslav Pelikan.

God's sense of timing, place, "coincidence" always stuns me. While writing in Bratislava, Slovakia, I read the writings of Pelikan, famed professor of theology at Yale Divinity School. Pelikan was the son of a Lutheran pastor from, as it happened, Bratislava. His take on Jesus through the ages and our human yearning to know him more deeply is compelling.

In *The Illustrated Jesus Through the Centuries*, Pelikan, like Dr. Allen, offers an array of conceptual Jesuses. Pelikan writes that Jesus has been perceived as "The Turning Point of History, Cosmic Christ, King of Kings, Son of Man, Light of the Gentiles, The True Image, The Christ Crucified, The Monk Who Ruled the World, The Model Exemplar, Universal Man, Prince of Peace, Teacher of Common Sense, Liberator, The Man Who Belongs to the World." Plus, my favorites, "The Bridegroom of the Soul, Poet of the Spirit, Mirror of the Eternal."

To explain all these variations, however outlandish, Pelikan reminds us that the Bible teaches that Jesus is "the same yesterday, today and tomorrow" (Hebrews 13:8). Yet, he adds, "each successive epoch found its own thoughts in Jesus which was, indeed, the only way in which it could make him live," for typically one "created

Are We Bored Yet? The Jesus Quest

him in accordance with one's character" (*The Illustrated Jesus Through the Centuries*, p.2). In accordance with one's character. Or needs.

That doesn't mean that we are free to create Jesus in our own image. It does mean that we are free to dig deep, deep and even deeper into the Jesus of history to understand how this "Word made flesh" (John 1:14) has flesh today. This is not a game. This is life, mortal and eternal.

I took a course at Harvard Divinity School on the history of Christian religion in war. When we came to World War I we read battlefield reports from the French and German soldiers. Though most all were baptized Christians, they were slaughtering each other in the trenches. But they weren't too busy to not see God at work for their side, with apparitions of Jesus and Mary and intervention of angels, God's minions orchestrating the massacre of the other guys.

We want Jesus to be on our side, not only to like us but to be like us. But how far can we take this personalization of Jesus according to our whims and fancies, prejudices and needs, our own character?

In a course I took with Harvey Cox, Cox presented a slideshow of images of Jesus from Latin America, created during its most revolutionary years. From gruesome to colorful to overtly political, Jesus was portrayed in the daily life of the poor and the oppressed.

One image Cox showed us was notable for its rejection by the people. It depicted Jesus in the uniform of a revolutionary, holding an AK-47, his chest

My Jesus

crisscrossed with a bandolier of bullets. The popular idea of Zapata or Che Guevara, superimposed on Jesus. This image appeared widely on posters as a marketing tool, equating the Jesus everyone worshipped with the revolution that was underway. But the people wouldn't have it. As fast as the posters were put up, they were torn down. That Jesus was unacceptable – even during an epoch of revolution.

We hear about Jesus as Shaman – Madman – Feminist – Revolutionary, along with King of Kings – Lord of Lords – Prince of Peace. We add in Messiah-Christ – Salvator Mundi and it begins to feel like all the "Jesus Searchers" (Charlotte Allen's phrase) live in different universes. We are all back in kindergarten, as the teacher points at the blackboard where it is written 2+2 = ?, and each of us eagerly raises our hand to shout out a vastly different number. Doesn't anyone see four? Or at least my four?

Schweitzer, the guru of the endless quest for a true Jesus, called Jesus "a failure, but a dazzling failure," almost as if failure was the goal. To explain, he offers this disturbing image:

"Jesus, the coming Son of Man, lays hold of the wheel of the world to set it moving on that last revolution which is to bring all ordinary history to a close. It refuses to turn, and he throws Himself upon it. Then it does turn and crushes him. The wheel rolls onward, and the mangled body of the one immeasurably Great Man, who was strong enough to think of himself as the one spiritual ruler of mankind and to bend history to his purpose, is hanging upon it still. That is His victory and His reign" (Allen, *The Human Christ*, p.238; Schweitzer, *Quest for the Historical Jesus*, p. 368-9).

Yet that very same Schweitzer abandoned multiple lucrative careers in Europe to pursue a life of sacrifice as a medical missionary in Gabon, in service to that dead and mangled body stripped of all wonder. There is something compelling about Jesus, however demythologized and brought back to earth.

Are we bored yet? Or depressed? Let a Bratislavan save the day. Pelikan famously said, "If Christ is risen, nothing else matters. And if Christ is not risen – nothing else matters." Christ, my Jesus, always matters.

But to what degree do I have the right to personalize Jesus? To what degree should we be digging, asking, turning upside down and inside out? This can sound like some modernist, liberal, academic version of how many angels can dance on the head of a pin. Once again, Pelikan says it better. "To invoke Kierkegaard's figure of speech, the beauty of the language of the Bible can be like a set of dentist's instruments laid out on a table and hanging on a wall, intriguing in their technological complexity and with their stainless steel highly polished – until they set to work on the job for which they were originally designed. Then all of a sudden, my reaction changes from 'How shiny and beautiful they all are!' to 'Get that damned thing out of my mouth!'" (Jaroslav Pelikan, 2006, *Whose Bible Is It?* p.229, Penguin).

But sometimes we need a dentist. A good root canal at the right time makes a world of difference, as does

My Jesus

Novocaine, teeth cleaning, or filling a cavity. Our Jesus-ology, if there is such a word, can use all the dentist's tools. We don't need to be afraid or offended. Jesus can handle it.

Perhaps you have smiled along with me and rolled your eyes at some of the efforts listed to reimagine Jesus through the epochs. My eyes continue to roll at the not-my-Jesus presented on a daily basis: Christian TV, Facebook posts, news stories constantly besmirch the Jesus I adore.

After 9/11, well-intentioned religious people hastened to smooth over interfaith fractures by proclaiming "we all worship the same God." I was one of those folks. But being repelled by spokespersons in my own religion has emboldened me to say, when necessary, to all kinds of so-called believers, "That is not my God," and even "That is not my Jesus."

On YouTube I heard a Christian pastor, after lambasting gay people, proclaim with a glint in his eye, "I am not talking about executing gay people … yet." On a Christian TV channel, a popular preacher was describing to his Sunday congregation in gory detail the suffering awaiting non-Christians after they die, and his Sunday morning worshippers were cheering, guffawing, rejoicing. I grew up at a time and in a way when the threat of Hell was real, which motivated us to love our neighbor and stranger even more. Now Hell elicits wild applause at the thought of neighbors, strangers, and family members enduring eternal torment. Nope, that's not my God.

And I've lost track of the times someone sends out an inspiring Facebook post, a beautiful Bible verse, a soothing spiritual picture, followed by a scathing and ugly tirade against half of America. It's like, "God bless you, you moronic, traitorous jerk." Gee, thanks. Their Jesus is far removed from any semblance of Jesus I adore.

The Jesus I adore won't be caught dead cheering the execution of gay people, the miseries of the damned, or the insults tossed at half a nation. These anti-Jesus Jesuses require a complete challenge. I volunteer to do it.

To write, to preach, to think, to live is to fully embrace today with a respectful nod to yesterday. The tug between the traditions of the past and the realities of the present should be exciting, not threatening.

Once again, it is Pelikan to the rescue. On the occasion of his eightieth birthday he wrote, "Tradition is the living faith of dead people to which we must add our chapter while we have the gift of life. Traditionalism is the dead faith of living people who fear that if anything changes, the whole enterprise will crumble…Tradition lives in conversation with the past, while remembering where we are and when we are and that it is we who have to decide. Traditionalism supposes that nothing should ever be done for the first time. (*Orthodoxy and Western Culture: A Collection of Essays honoring Jaroslav Pelikan on His Eightieth Birthday,* p.16, St. Vladmir's Seminary Press).

The conceit of any author or preacher is that they have something new to offer. Otherwise, one could

My Jesus

simply put "ditto, blah, blah, blah, etc." between two covers and call it a book. With this book I add my chapter to the traditions of a living faith, allowing me to stay in conversation with dead people who have shaped Jesus before me and for me.

I once wrote a book about work. It was my theology of work, a reflection on the meaning of vocation. I thought it was good. A month later Donald Hall, the legendary poet and Connecticut Yankee, came out with a better book. When I wrote to tell him that he had written the book I wished I'd written, he was gracious and complimentary. I knew better. His was better.

In writing about Jesus, I join a huge parade of authors. My only defense is that this is my story, the story of my lifelong walk with Jesus. In addition, anyone's story is lived within a context. That context shapes the Jesus we learn, the Jesus we know, the Jesus we embrace, the Jesus we share.

The Gospels of Matthew, Mark, Luke and John were the first attempt to write down "My Jesus," and that was over 1900 years ago. Scholars, novelists, artists, hymn writers, Broadway producers, song writers, preachers and Sunday School teachers have been adding their own versions, even if they don't call it that.

Whether it's Handel's "Messiah" with a hundred voice choir and a full orchestra proclaiming the Hallelujah Chorus, or the old song inviting you to "put your hand in the hand of the man who stilled the water," or a little New England congregation reminding each other that "In the Garden ... he walks with me, and talks with me, and tells me I am his own," each is saying, "let me tell you about my Jesus."

Broadway's "Jesus Christ, Superstar" contrasts an over-the-top title and title song with the plaintive and oh-so-truthful "I don't know how to love him."

The great religious art of the world's museums and the whole artistic explosion of Europe's grand churches offer a spectacular breadth of understanding. My Jesus can be an idyllic cherub sitting on Mary's lap, holding the world in the palm of his tiny hand, an enthralling teacher who commands his audience, a man in awful agony on the cross, a gruesome dead body, an ethereal resurrected presence, or a universally triumphant spectre looming over the earth.

For one Good Friday service at our church, we created a video compilation of paintings portraying Jesus on the Cross. Each artist seemed to be saying to the viewer, "here is my Jesus, this is what he means to me, this is what I want you to know." Fra Angelico and El Greco and Rubens presented a Jesus obediently doing the dying he was meant to do. Titian and Matthias Grunewald made us feel the suffering. For William Blake, always working off his own visions, Jesus was submissive. Egon Schiele and Craigie Aitchison and even Munch showed Jesus abandoned, alone, forsaken. Graham Sutherland's cubist, fractured Jesus mirrored the worst of industrialization, all lived on one cross. For all of these, Christ's suffering was no passing moment on the way to resurrection. Yet for many artists, Jesus is transcendent even at what should be the worst moment

My Jesus

of his life. Chagall's Jesus is almost at peace. Nalini Jayasuriya, Soichi Watanabe and He Qi offer Jesus in such serenity that the victory of Easter is front and center even on Good Friday. Picasso and Dali bring us images of Jesus so strong and assured they really are above it all.

Our hymns do the same. Indeed, I am certain that a good psychologist or social historian would see a very clear connection between the hymns of my growing up years and the Jesus of my development. Hymn after hymn offers a Jesus who is relational, personal, intimate, involved; and describe a love so intense that it serves as the model for all human love.

Our three-hundred-year-old church, with one foot in ancient American history and one squarely in the 21st Century, begins each autumn with the entire Sunday School marching into a church full of waiting parents and grandparents and happy adults all singing "Jesus loves me this I know." It never grows old. The promise that "In the Garden" offers of a one-on-one encounter with Jesus is an adult version of the same sentiment, and through the year we'll add to it with "My Jesus, I love Thee, I know thou art mine," "What a Friend We Have in Jesus" and "Blessed Assurance, Jesus is Mine." Other hymns bind us together in purpose and service, fueled by that love. "All to Jesus I Surrender, I Surrender All," "Jesus Calls Us O'er the Tumult," "Christ for the World We Sing." First on Broadway and then in local musical theaters worldwide, Godspell's "Day by Day" lays out this Jesus-hymn theology with a folk twist perfect for the era:

>   Day by day, Day by day

> Oh, Dear Lord
> Three things I pray
> To see thee more clearly
> Love thee more dearly
> Follow thee more nearly
> Day by day
> > ("Day by Day," from *Godspell*, Schwartz 1972)

That is the perfect addendum to "Jesus Loves Me." Jesus loves me; therefore, I want to see, love and follow him to a richer, fuller level than ever experienced before.

There is a triumphant voice to some Jesus hymns, certainly. "Jesus shall Reign Where'er the Sun" makes "Crown Him with Many Crowns" perfect sense.

One Easter night I was invited to a Pentecostal church for their Easter musical extravaganza. After a powerful, visual retelling of Jesus' death and resurrection, from gruesome cross to empty tomb and marveling disciples, the culmination was a victorious monarch's dream. With Jesus sitting on a golden throne, the potentates of every nation process to the throne, dozens in fine robes with trailing servants, bowing, offering their own crowns, presenting gifts worthy of, well, of the King. You could hear Handel's emphatic "Hallelujah Chorus" in your head:

> King of Kings
> And Lord of Lords.
> King of Kings
> And Lord of Lords.
> And he shall reign forever and ever.
> And ever.

My Jesus

> And ever.
> And ever.
> Hallelujah! Hallelujah!! Hallelujah!!!
> Halle-lu-jah!!

And it felt good. At my competitive best (or worst) it can feel good to imagine that all the world's skeptics and doubters and naysayers and opponents, and everyone who spent their career demythologizing Jesus – all those people will be standing there, slack jawed, stunned silent, experiencing their own shock and awe. And we get to say "See? I told you so!" Adolescent, I know.

Yet absent the crass smugness, to know we were right, that the "Jesus, Friend, So Kind and Gentle," who lived the humblest life of the truest suffering servant, is finally recognized and gets his due from all the world – yes, that could be a good moment.

But what gets me to that moment is more the "In the Garden" experience than the "Crown Him with Many Crowns" promise. I need to know he is my Jesus, and from that bond I follow him.

My wife (and co-pastor) Alida Ward and I are rock fans, she for Bruce Springsteen, me for Green Day. We've both been to many concerts together, with both bands. With tens of thousands of others. Yet after every concert, on the way home, one of us will say to the other, "did you notice when he sang that song looking right at you?! That was so special." And we believe it.

My faith is that personal. My Jesus is that personal. My church is that personal. That's how I like it. That's how I need it.

Without exaggeration, the hymn guiding my spirit while writing this chapter is that personal. "My Jesus, I Love Thee":

> My Jesus I love thee,
> I know thou art mine;
> for thee all the follies
> of sin I resign;
> my gracious Redeemer,
> my savior art thou;
> if ever I loved thee,
> my Jesus 'tis now.
> I love thee because
> thou hast first loved me,
> and purchased my pardon
> on Calvary's tree;
> I love thee for wearing
> the thorns on thy brow;
> if ever I loved thee,
> my Jesus 'tis now.
>
> ("My Jesus, I Love Thee,"
> William Ralph Featherstone, 1864)

TWO

My Journey With Jesus

I was sent away to boarding school shortly after my 13th birthday. That's how it was put in those days: "sent away to boarding school." Nobody in my neighborhood knew what boarding school was, exactly. Reform School we knew, because of the older young hoods, the kids in my gang that got caught. Prison we knew, for uncles and cousins, and neighbors who disappeared. One day you're in the neighborhood, the next day you're not. But boarding school? Even I had no idea what I was heading to.

Who knew it would be a thousand acres of pristine woods in the idyllic Berkshires, founded by America's most famous evangelist? At the Mount Hermon School for Boys, we were required to play sports and be with our friends, without parents around, and with seconds for dinner. It was more than a fair trade-off for the equally mandatory work, chapel and Bible courses. A good life.

My parents were more anxious. Along with the five dollars in spending money to last until Thanksgiving, they gave me a framed picture of Jesus. Just Jesus, not doing anything in particular, more like posing for a photo, looking straight ahead.

Coming from a very Christian family and now being at a very Christian school, I put the framed Jesus on my desk. The next day, when I came back from class, Jesus had been moved from my desk. I put him back in his place, but the next day it happened again. And again. Every day I would return to my room from sports, class, meal, date or punishment detail and Jesus would be somewhere else. Sometimes upside down, or on his side, or behind books, or stuffed in the closet. Jesus was my Elf on a Shelf long before that was a thing.

Clearly my roommate was the culprit. But as a thirteen-year-old city kid stuck with a stranger, I wasn't sure how to confront him about Jesus-stealing, or Jesus-moving, or Jesus-envy.

My roommate finally told me, right after my father made a surprise visit and couldn't find my Jesus. "The eyes," my roommate confessed, "his eyes follow me wherever I go. So first I turned him upside down, but then he looked angry." "Look," he said, taking my Jesus and turning him upside down on my desk. Sure enough, he looked angry. And sure enough, when I thought about it, everywhere I went in the room, Jesus had been looking at me. Intensely, if he was upright, as if very interested. Angry, if he had been disrespected in some move.

What does this story teach? Well, at that stage of my life Jesus was very real. He was on top of things. He was capable of attitude. He followed you.

I know that liberal academia is accused by many of shaking faith, if not destroying it, but I don't believe that. Bad faith kills faith. Bad church, bad religion, bad clergy, bad dogma kill faith. I am now way beyond thirteen. New England Prep School, courses in world religions, mandatory college 101 and core courses, the guest speakers and campus movements and social unrest of my liberal academia life are well behind me.

None of that killed my faith. Jesus is still real, still on top of things, still follows me, and still is more than capable of attitude.

I come about my relationship with Jesus the hard way, by working at it my whole life. My father and I had similar faith journeys. We grew up in homes where Christian faith and activity were always present, never on the sideline. That doesn't mean we always followed. But it, and him, always followed us.

Raised in a home where Jesus was part of the family, it was clear that everything was viewed through the prism of faith in general, and of Jesus in particular. Decades later, visiting a family in their home, I saw an embroidered wall hanging that stated:

> *Jesus is the Head of this Home*
> *The Unseen Guest at every Meal*
> *The Silent Listener to every Conversation.*

We didn't have that sign in our house, but we lived it. I might take issue with the "unseen" and "silent" part, because Jesus was very much a presence. It was assumed that he knew everything going on, wanted a say in it, might wait for an invitation to join in, or not wait.

Our family history, up to this very day, is strangely complex and uniquely focused. The complex part is that we wander all over the place, far beyond the bounds of traditional Protestantism. The focused part is Jesus.

My Journey With Jesus

Our fervent Christianity began with my grandfather's conversion as a young man. A brutal and accomplished street brawler, a baseball star whom the pros were following, dirt poor from a hardscrabble Maine farming family, God took hold of him and Jesus took ownership. That was that, the end of baseball and brawling. The brand of Christianity that saved him literally never took its eye off Jesus, peering intently at the heavens, awaiting his return. For Linwood Rowe's Advent Christian faith, it was all about what Jesus did when he was here the first time, and what Jesus would do when he came back. Linwood and Elsie's four children devoted their entire lives to Jesus Christ, in one form or another. New ways, new wrinkles, new emphases. Same Jesus: alive, present, interested, involved. That was our Saving Grace, no matter what else crept into our religious practice. My father, Gard, left the Advent Christian denomination to seek Christian practice more focused on justice in the present, not just heaven in the future. He would not wait for Christ's second coming to get Christ's Kingdom up and running in the here and now. "Thy Kingdom come, thy will be done on earth as it is in heaven," Jesus taught us to pray (Matthew 6:10); anything Jesus taught was to be taken at face value. My father never lost sight of Jesus and his heaven nor of the world he gave his life for on the cross. This world must be important, he figured.

He and my grandfather, uncles and cousins, spouses and children, have 300 years of church ministry that never lost sight of Jesus. This spurred them to help the poor, stand up for justice, feed the hungry, work for peace, preach, evangelize, convert, reconcile, heal. They

My Jesus

were immersed in the church, the world, the community, the sacred spaces and the dark places. Alida and I add many more years and many new wrinkles. Civil rights, LGBTQ Rights, Women's Rights, Human Rights are causes rooted in our very understanding of Jesus, not inspite of or aside from. We travel down ecumenical and interfaith paths my grandfather never imagined, but my father explored. Our stance is that we'll take Jesus anywhere. Sometimes it is more like Jesus will take us anywhere. Either way, like Jesus in my dorm room, he will not be turned upside down, disrespected, or hidden away without challenge. With us, you get Jesus.

But what Jesus? Which Jesus?

We are the products of our environment. Home, family, neighborhood, school, nation, church, generation, era, economy, health. Yet I want to believe that my Jesus is rock steady, transferable to every age and place and condition. I do believe it. But the touchstones of that Jesus-faith are from the worlds I know. Today's world is scarily more confrontational, dogmatic, nationalistic, divided and divisive, alienated and alien, insulting, tyrannical, and blasphemous in its hatred. Much of that is driven by religion of some sort.

Every religion in our contemporary times has a fringe wing capable of the worst behaviors, outliers who are an embarrassment to that religion, its founder and scriptures and values. The Christ of a lot of Christians is unrecognizable when immersed in hate. A famous photographer, Andres Serrano, got in a lot of trouble for presenting an artwork of the crucified Christ immersed in urine. There are Christians now sinking Christ in a lot worse. Meanwhile, religiously our world has moved toward the extremes: atheism and apathy in one corner, my way or the highway fundamentalism in the other. Like a boxing match, at any moment the bell will ring, and each fighter must lurch from their corner to duke it out. Low blows are not only allowed but encouraged.

That's today's landscape, political, spiritual, social, even familial.

Does my Jesus speak to that? Or is he sidelined for now? Out of touch? Of another time? Too old fashioned? Or biding his time?

My recent writings are filled with central European stories of Prague, Krakow, Bratislava. I could easily add Florence, Paris, Madrid. My earlier writings were equally fueled by Africa, India and Central America, for the same reason. If you step outside yourself, your comfort zone, your routine, you may see things in fresh ways.

Bratislava has been great fun. We've taken each other to heart, thanks especially to the Franciscan church about ten feet from my hotel. They have welcomed me, inspired, fed and enriched me. That connection led to fifteen Catholic priests and young people staying at our church in Connecticut for several days on the way to see the Pope in Panama. Naturally, when Alida and I next travelled to Bratislava they gave us a splendid welcome. During an abundant dinner I used them as a focus group for this book, grilling them about what Jesus meant to them in their world, in this age, with these situations and their own unique sufferings under Nazis and

My Jesus

Communists. They loved the question, and our conversation took off in many different directions. At one point I asked about their church, a 13th Century amalgamation of styles that catch your eye everywhere you look. Over on the side is the preserved body of Saint Reparatus, a deacon killed for Christ in the 4th Century, lying in sweet repose. Above him is a raised pulpit typical of ancient churches, ornately decorated. And from the side of the pulpit, a disembodied arm sticks out, holding a large crucifix.

Good dinnertime talk, I thought, so I inquired: What is the lone arm with the crucifix jutting out from the pulpit all about?

Father Joseph said that back in the 1300's Jesus was viewed as supreme royalty, triumphant, victorious, crowned, regal, accompanied by all the accoutrements of monarchy. He was the King of Kings, no doubt.

In that epoch, at that time, Saint Francis came along and declared to all would-be Franciscans that they must preach what people needed to know: Christ crucified, and resurrected. He didn't care what was trendy, popular, accepted, visually pleasing or easy preaching. His Jesus had been crucified; his Jesus had a love for the world so great that he would hold nothing back. His Jesus gave it all. Thus, the arm holding a cross sticking out from the pulpit.

That gave me the answer to what Jesus is, the Jesus whom I boldly and proudly present to a terribly conflicted world. The crucified and risen Christ, for sure. But it also reminded me that what I strongly, urgently, passionately feel is the heart of Jesus is surely relevant to every epoch. Saint Francis was not saying to the Catholic Church, "Look, the Royal Jesus with the pomp and circumstance, scepter and globe was fine in its time, but let's do Christ crucified for a generation or two. Balance, you know."

No. Francis was saying that there are many aspects of Jesus, many levels of understanding, many emphases worth highlighting from time to time. But certain parts are eternal, never to be forgotten.

The Jesus I present is certainly the Jesus of my lifetime, the Jesus of my environment, the Jesus of my epoch. But it is not a trend, a fad, some useful tool for today that may fade in tomorrow's Christianity, and never surfaced in yesterday's. I haven't discovered something. I've tapped into something.

For every Christian whose faith resounds deeply in their daily life, there is often one scripture story that never leaves them. One story that never leaves me is the one known as "The Second Touch" (Mark 8:22-26).

Jesus arrived at a village where some compassionate people bring a blind man for him to "touch." The rest of this healing story is intriguing and instructive. In short order, Jesus "leads him outside the village ... spits on the man's eyes and put his hands on him" (vs.23). The result is both wonderful and imperfect. "I see people," the man says gratefully, I'm sure. "They look like trees walking." In other words, the man gets some sight, but things aren't clear. That's plenty good enough for the blind man. That's not good enough for Jesus.

My Jesus

Jesus reaches out a second time, touching the man's eyes a second time, taking an already stunning miracle to a second level, deeper, surer, complete. "His sight was restored," Mark tells us, "and he saw everything clearly" (vs.25).

Here you have Jesus, a person in need, friends who care, an unorthodox approach, an okay result, a do-over, and an end result worth celebrating. Like all of Jesus' miracles, this one is provocative and helpful, an easy story to build upon. What am I blind to? How do I stumble around in the dark? Who is there to guide me? Why don't I see people clearly? Why do some people look to me like sticks, not real people? Why do I settle for half measures, given and received? Who don't I really want to see, anyway? Why is seeing clearly something I avoid? How blind can I be? Do I even want to see clearly? Or is seeing people as inanimate objects good enough for me?

Jesus is never happy with what others would be willing to settle for or pass off as okay. Even his idiosyncratic actions are designed to provoke us to think and act in deeper ways. Why does Jesus take the blind man by the hand and lead him outside the village before initiating any healing action? Or is that part of the healing? And what do we make of Jesus "spitting on the man's eyes"?

At the very least they show that Jesus will do whatever it takes to save a life, change a life, make a difference.

Once again, each is a statement. Sometimes to be healed, changed, saved, to see clearly, we need to be taken out of our comfort zone. Redirection, change of pace, fresh perspective, surprise. Jesus constantly surprises. In this instance he has the person he's helping, the blind man, walk with him "outside the village." Oftentimes we need to put certain things behind us. Old ways, old habits, even old friends may need to be left.

When I finally succeeded in quitting pipe smoking after forty years, the key was not throwing away the pipes or flushing tobacco down the toilet. I had to literally move out of my favorite room, give away my favorite desk, store away my favorite chair. Like the blind man, I had to be removed from what was.

As for the spit? In our times, that sounds both unpleasant and unhygienic. But my mother always promoted the healing powers inherent in spit. When I was out playing, away from home and the medicine cabinet, if I got a scrape or wound, I was taught to spit on it, rub it in.

Scholars go further, suggesting that spit was thought of as coming from within us, something inherent to us, of our essence. Jesus called forth his essence from within to make the deepest connection with the blind man.

Isn't Jesus saying that a significant feature of healing is to call upon every aspect of our full self, hold nothing back, offer our essence in the effort? And also, get away from what's holding us back?

This "Second Touch" story is striking also for its resemblance to other teachings and healings. You have to think Jesus was making a point. Later in the Gospels, when Jesus reconciled with Peter, what did Jesus do?

Repeat himself. "Do you love me?" he asked Peter. And he asks again. And again. Three asks to match, reverse, erase Peter's infamous three denials of Jesus earlier.

Over and over again, Jesus constantly stays on course with us, refuses to give up on anyone. I am convinced that if Judas had not killed himself, Jesus would have found a way to call him forward, stiffen his spine, clear his sight, heal his soul, and put him to work. There would be St. Judas churches all over the place, and I would be lighting candles in them.

Remember, all but one of the disciples abandoned Jesus at his darkest hour, the crucifixion. Even on Easter morning the remaining disciples refused to believe the resurrection story reported by the women, mocking them. Yet they were all welcomed back into the fold, including Thomas who, yes, needed a second touch.

On Easter afternoon, on the road to Emmaus, an incognito Jesus appears to two other distraught followers. They had been in Jerusalem for all the Holy Week drama and had heard rumors of the resurrection. Yet they despaired, could not bring themselves to believe such a story. So, they were headed back home, broken and discouraged. It's over.

Oh no, it is not over. It is never over with Jesus. Once, twice, whatever it takes. Jesus finds those two depressed, hopeless, discouraged men, their faith in tatters, and patiently gives them a second chance to believe.

The Gospels are full of men and women who tested the limits of grace and life itself, only to learn that with Christ there are no limits to grace or life itself.

Paul starts off his religious career killing Christians. Zacchaeus spent his life cheating people. Martha whined about having to do the dirty work. The so-called "good thief" was on the cross for being a "bad thief." The Samaritan woman was on her sixth husband. And Lazarus was actually dead.

None of that got in the way of Jesus' touch.

And you want THE clincher?

Forgive me for being graphic. Jesus, on the cross, after hours of torture, slowly and excruciatingly being asphyxiated while bleeding out, nails in hands and feet, mocked and jeered by the crowd, feeling abandoned by God, bearing the sins of the world, innocent of every charge, says "Father, forgive them for they know not what they do" (Luke 23:34).

Them? Who are they? The "them" would be anyone complicit in his death. Roman government and their soldiers. Jewish religious authorities and their minions. The crowd who loved executions and gore. The disciples hovering in a corner somewhere. The crowds who lined the street in silence to give Rome what it wanted. Judas who sold him out. Peter who denied him. All the folks in Jerusalem that week who waved palms when he rode by, and cheered his every word and deed, then vanished behind closed doors and shut windows and tight mouths. The thief who mocked him. The soldier who pounded the nails. The soldiers who forced the crown of thorns down tight on his head until he bled. The Pharisees and citizens and followers who knew full well, at the least, that he was innocent.

My Jesus

That was then. This is now. Now requires a theological jump from "them" to "us." In those awful moments of bitter anguish on the cross, Jesus certainly forgives the "them" literally accomplishing his anguish. But the larger purpose of the cross, the object, the reason is us.

As we did for "them" it is fair to define "us". If Jesus dies on the cross "for God so loved the world" and wants us forgiven of our sins, then just as certainly we are the *us* <u>and</u> the *them.* Every time we miss the mark of Christlikeness it is a contributing factor to Jesus' anguish on the cross. Every sin or failure or disappointment in light of God's best hopes for us, however grand or picayune, is one more pounding of the nail through the flesh of Jesus into the wood of the cross. Perhaps that is too much to imagine. But how else can we weigh the magnificence of Jesus' "Second Touch" that enables us to see and live clearly, now and eternally?

That is my Jesus. The Jesus of my church. The Jesus of my epoch. The Jesus of the "second touch" upon the "us" within "them."

But I didn't find him by myself. It is a family trait. The "second touch" story itself is two thousand years old, foundational enough to the basic Christian story to have made it into the Gospels. It has been emulated in every epoch. But in my personal journey it has been front and center.

My grandfather Linwood was an old-fashioned preacher with what was called a "tentmaker" ministry. That term comes from St. Paul who really was a tentmaker and would use his trade to pay the bills when he was on the road evangelizing the Mediterranean. Grandpa was a master carpenter by trade, and he plied that trade his entire sixty-plus year career as a preacher. He literally built one church, constructing it Monday through Friday while preaching and pastoring on the weekends and evenings.

His claim to fame was his second touch healing ministry. He had an uncanny ability to save alcoholics, street bums, the town drunk, the functioning alcoholics, the silent and hidden ones, the ones who lost everything or never had anything – they were his most unique calling.

Anyone with experience with addiction of any kind knows that recovery, healing, wholeness is never a one-off. It is most assuredly a process. A second touch. A second second touch. Maybe ten second touches. Or maybe Jesus wasn't exaggerating when he said "seventy times seven." Four hundred and ninety is a big number. For most people with friends and loved ones in the throes of addiction, two is a big number.

Giving someone a second chance, second touch, can be a gamble, with risks and costs: emotional, financial, relational, even safety and health and family well-being. But my grandfather, my father, my Uncle Gerald and Lloyd, all pastors, were all masters of the second touch. None of them gave up on anybody. That was the understanding of ministry I grew up with, watching them in action, listening to their stories, knowing their commitment even to me. I was the full beneficiary of seventy times seven.

It is this personal connection that has resulted in my using the personal pronoun, naming Jesus as "my" Jesus. To me it is an added blessing that Jesus can be experienced personally, even uniquely. Evangelical Christians have long asked others, "do you know Jesus?", and more pointedly, "do you have a personal relationship with Jesus?" It definitely was off-putting, however it may have been intended. It seemed to imply, "hey, my faith is real, yours isn't; my Jesus is my friend, yours is whatever." Sadly, lots of Christians do this. If you don't speak in tongues, pray to Mary, read the King James Version of the Bible, lift your arms while singing, tithe, go to the correct church, vote the right way, then, prima facie, you're not a true Christian. Everyone has a litmus test, like whether or not Jesus is your best bud.

Nevertheless, the desire to initiate you into a closer, more intimate, more direct relationship with Jesus is a supremely noble and loving desire. Take it at face value and forget the tone or condescension or judgmentalism that comes with it.

Very likely, you are a fan of somebody – a particular athlete, star, rock band, author, hero. If you were offered the chance to meet them, you would take it.

Jesus wants to be met. What's better, Jesus is perfectly willing to meet on your terms. Your turf. More than halfway. Jesus wants to meet.

That's certainly the best summary of my personal journey with Jesus. Chance meetings, planned meetings, surprise meetings, close encounters of the third kind, in your face, mediator, loud, stream of consciousness, visual, sensory, tactile, outdoors, indoors, church, art museum, concert, forest, praying, running, weeping.

Always, there was Jesus.

This is not to suggest I was always spiritual, faithful, aware, responsive or worthy. I wouldn't have sought me out. But I have always been sought after. That is the M.O. of my Jesus.

One Sunday, in place of the sermon, we had a young actor in our church present Francis Thompson's "The Hound of Heaven." This epic poem shows God as the title character, the hound who relentlessly pursues us, never quitting, never lagging in zeal, never losing interest.

Jesus is the embodiment of God's hounding persistence. It is not always welcome, or convenient. It is always. The Christian bumper sticker is correct: "I Love You. And There's Absolutely Nothing You Can Do About It."

If Jesus is the embodiment of God's hounding obsession, if he is the "near end of God," (my favorite expression, from Wolfhart Pannenberg), if he is God's word made flesh to dwell among us, then it is Christ's people who are to be the embodiment of Jesus. Those who choose the name Christian, those who choose the Church as homebase, those who choose to be Christlike, our job is to be God's word made flesh now.

My Jesus is the absolute direct result of churches and church people embodying Jesus to such a degree that I

My Jesus

wanted to be like them and like him. They did their job. That is evangelism. In the words of a classic Christian phrase, they "brought me to Jesus," introducing me to this Jesus who is ever and ever more crisply defined.

As a Protestant child in the 50s, I was introduced to the Jesus of flannelgraph, film strips, Sunday School Bible-based comics. We thought we were cutting edge. On a good Sunday we could silently read our comic book Bible lesson. Then the teacher went to the flannelgraph board and moved around cut-out figures to recreate the Biblical story. If we were lucky, the story would then come alive on the big screen via film strip, each staged scene projecting some Biblical reality behind our faith.

My churches, from childhood through fifty years of pastoring, have been filled with people who brought Biblical scenes to life and lived Christlike faith fully. Going the extra mile for me, turning the other cheek for me, forgiving seventy times seven for me. Being bold and creative and risk taking in ministry. Visionary in mission. Jesus said, "Pick up your cross," and they did. Jesus, after washing his disciples' feet, said "I've set you an example, do as I have done," and they did. Jesus said "go ye into all the world," and they did. Jesus said to honor the smallest penny, reach out to the least and worst and the unlikeliest, and they did. Jesus found ways to heal, time to pray, strength to listen, and they did. Jesus confronted Satan, dismissed demons, recognized evil, and so did they. Jesus was the Hound of Heaven, and they most certainly were. Are.

My Journey With Jesus

A favorite but often overlooked part of the Christmas story, among some Protestants, is the depth of Mary's role. We get that she was the mom. Some of us still believe in the Virgin Birth. But far more miraculous is her response to God overwhelming her life. First, she tells the angel Gabriel, "I am the Lord's servant. May it be to me as you have said." Or, okay, fine (Luke 1:38). Second, later, when she meets up with her cousin, Elizabeth, Mary proclaims, "My soul magnifies the Lord." (Luke 1:46) What a sterling and bold declaration. Imagine living with the determination to magnify God, to make God larger and clearer and more distinct. That is what a magnifying glass does. That is what Mary promised and delivered. That is what generations of church people, church leaders and loved ones have done for me. The Jesus I adore and offer was magnified by them.

Magnifying the Lord is a tall order and takes new courage every age. Some time ago I was asked to consider pastoring a strong church in North Carolina. An esteemed Biblical scholar, Robert Bratcher, was on the Search Committee. Bob told me, "we will never ask you why you did something. We will surely ask you why you didn't." Jesus constantly moved forward, lifted people up, saw a path beyond, knew there was hope. Jesus never sat idly by.

"Christian Formation" is a popular term now. But for me it has been "Jesus Formation," seeing Jesus lived and practiced as if he were right there, here, in the middle of it all.

My Jesus

Some of that emanated from unlikely pop culture sources. My father had his own version of home-schooling. If there was something I should see or experience or take part in, his face would appear at the window of my P.S. 90 classroom, and I'd be whisked away for an adventure. I met military heroes at Fort Hamilton, fed the city's drunks at the Bowery Rescue Mission, visited the severely and imprisoned insane at Creedmore, took in a day game at Yankee Stadium. One day we drove into Manhattan, to some old-timey grand theatre, for the Italian, award-winning movie, "The Gospel According to St. Matthew." That was an eye-opener. The Jesus of my little Queens church Sunday School, off the flannelgraph, up on the biggest screen I had ever seen, in Manhattan, the capitol of the universe. This Jesus was not only giant-size and award-winning, he was fervent, dogged, powerful, in command, compelling. My Jesus, afresh.

Film and Broadway kept at it, evangelism for Jesus that was profound. "Godspell" and "The Cotton-Patch Gospel," on and off Broadway, gave us Jesus filled with humor, poignancy, vigor, purpose. The Jesus of our greatest hopes, greatest fears, greatest doubts, greatest works was all there. Make of it what you will. "Jesus Christ Superstar" didn't back away from Jesus, Christ or Superstar, and all those names each imply.

In my early ministry I made wide use of avant-garde short films that fleshed out Jesus in ways that kept you awake a long time. In "The Carpenter" a young carpenter physically carries the cross he's built across a beleaguered and cynical city to a beleaguered church and pastor, stopped along the way by a little child asking the only sentence in the film, "Mister, are you Jesus?"

"The Parable," first shown at the 1964 World's Fair, offers substitutionary atonement in the form of a circus clown who takes the place of every broken, abused, exhausted co-worker, all the way to his death. And unlikely resurrection. Or is it unlikely?

In the first chapter of this book, I described the many attempts to demythologize Jesus. My concern was that it seemed that they started with an end game already decided. It was as if someone declared that it is time to get rid of any Jesus material that is supernatural, or forces us to think, or makes us wonder with awe.

My Jesus is more the result of reimagining. This is creative, expansive, provocative, exciting.

On Broadway years ago, I saw the great British actor Alec McGowan present "The Gospel of Mark." It was plain and simple. McGowan, a table, a chair, a bottle of water, a glass. And then, word for word, the ancient Gospel of Jesus as written by an almost disciple, Mark. In writing this chapter I re-read an old New York Times review from 1974. Mostly laudatory, with some complaints, the reviewer highlights McGowan's use of mime, facial expressions, all the crafts of a great stage actor. What I never forgot, and I can see in my mind's eye this very instant, is when Mark's Gospel moves from the overall narrative of Jesus' ministry to the really earth-moving, incendiary final acts of Jesus' life. Alec McGowan stood up, erect, and rolled up his sleeves. That said it all. The real work was about to begin.

Among the descriptive names, snide comments and honorific titles for Jesus, one of my favorites is a concept: Exemplar. It is both true of Jesus and one that we can aspire to. Bridegroom of the Soul, King of Kings, and Cosmic Christ are beyond me. But Exemplar he was, Exemplar we can be, Exemplars I have had aplenty. The Jesus of my life's journey is their gift to me.

The church I grew up in, the churches I've gone to, the churches I've pastored, the church people I've seen in action, the creative output of people vested in Jesus through art and film and music, and those whose lives so firmly resemble the clearest of Christlikeness – these are my Jesus in the making.

I will put this chapter to rest with the story of a couple who lived this to the fullest. My work with Habitat took me to India in 1983 where I met two Christian leaders, K. Azariah and Sister Mary Seethamma. They first taught me the term "Christlike," and embodied it so fully that it became the fundamental word of my entire ministry. It is the one-word test by which I gauge every part of my daily life, church work, mission projects. Oh my, how far short I fall personally and professionally, but it is still the test of every waking moment.

A large part of its power comes from having seen Azariah and Sister Mary emulate Christlikeness under conditions that would send most Christians running for the hills. Instead, their entire lives were spent running headlong into every condition, circumstance and need, and India has a way of producing the fullest variety of each. With crushing need, extreme urgency, growing persecution, with never enough resources from fickle donors and Western agencies who play with mission like a toy, these two produced miracle upon miracle straight from Jesus' book when he fed the multitudes with next to nothing. "Next to nothing is a lot," Azariah told me, without a hint of irony. I mean it, this was a mathematical equation for them. You take next to nothing, add the love of Jesus, you'll be amazed how much you have. Except they weren't amazed.

Lepers, beggars, orphans, outcasts, polio victims, amputees, elderly and child orphans, mentally handicapped youth, starving families, remote villagers, urban and town street dwellers, people overwhelmed by merely getting up in the morning with nothing to do, nowhere to go, no one to be with – that was their congregation. And the Jesus of their Christlikeness became the key to my Jesus. What more could you ask?

THREE
Jesus in the Bible

All Scripture is profitable. But some may be more helpful or agreeable.

I cut my teeth on the Bible. My bequeathed faith and my found faith take the Bible seriously. I hope that is what Paul, in his over-the-top way, was getting at when he said,

> All scripture is inspired by God (God-breathed) and is profitable (useful) for instruction/teaching, reproof, correction, and training in righteousness.
> (2 Timothy 3:16)

There are Christians, plenty of them, who take this to mean that God dictated every noun, verb and adjective to the various writers of the Bible, and that it is faithfully translated only in the King James version. No need for further translation or interpretation. It's all right there, clear as day, and if you have a problem with it take it up with God. That's the fundamentalist argument in the fundamentalist wing of every religion.

Taking Paul at his word, everything in the Bible is there for a reason: We can learn from it, be challenged or inspired, provoked or affirmed.

If we are honest, we all struggle with parts of the Bible. At this moment you could cite ten or twelve scripture verses or stories that you disagree with or find hard to believe. It might be the creation of the earth in six days, God destroying all the earth with Noah's flood and later Sodom and Gomorrah in fits of pique, God lighting Elijah's altar on fire after it was doused with water, Ezekiel calling the wind to breathe new life into the bones of dead soldiers. It could be Jesus raising Lazarus from the dead, Jesus casting out demons. We can add "blessed are the meek ... and they that mourn ... love never ends ... turn the other cheek."

Don't worry, the most ardent fundamentalist has a verse or two they stumble over. I have been in these conversations, each throwing verses at the other like some scriptural duel, each thinking they had the other in a box, each wiggling out of it with "yes, but." Even fundamentalists find themselves needing to contextualize verses at times.

Our context is to take scripture seriously, focusing on Jesus. To do that, there are three steps in the process. First, what did the Old Testament part of the Bible teach about the Messiah? What were the Jewish people waiting for when Jesus arrived on the scene?

Second, what did Jesus say about himself? Forget the Jesus Seminar stuff or Thomas Jefferson with his scissors, eliminating verses that they are certain Jesus would not have said. The four Gospels are the closest thing we have to contemporaneous biographies, and in their current state they have inspired believers for two millennia. In there is the Jesus who has dramatically impacted the world.

Third, what did the Christian Church start teaching about Jesus? With him effectively gone from the scene, the Church becomes his spokesperson, if you will. Their charge was to make sense of their Jesus for the wider world.

The first and third parts are the simplest. Jewish expectations for a Messiah were human and Divine. God promised them a Messiah. And they needed one badly. As a nation, Israel had prospered for a while. But with the passing of time Israel split apart and became easy prey for neighboring countries and would-be empires. Battles, wars, defeats, exile, and slavery resulted in a weakened Israel. From then on, they were passed from conqueror to conqueror, finally to Rome as "winner takes all." And Rome did.

Seven hundred years of military defeat and national humiliation left Israel dispirited and broken. They yearned for a hero, and God promised a Messiah. No doubt the two desires melded together.

The clearest expression of those desires is found in the famous verses of the Prophet Isaiah. When Christians gather to celebrate the Christmas birth of Jesus, our Christ, we find evidence that he is "the One" in many Old Testament verses. With the conviction of faith, we point to each as a proof that our Christian Jesus of Nazareth is properly the Jewish Messiah of prophecy. From birth in Bethlehem to burial in a borrowed grave, from birth to a virgin to an ignoble death, from riding a donkey into Jerusalem to being tempted by Satan, and even the thirty pieces of silver, these events point in a specific way to a specific person, and Jesus is the perfect match.

Jesus in the Bible

However, it is Isaiah's descriptions, made famous by Handel's "Messiah," that define the Jesus of prophecy. Isaiah's words are lofty and discouraging. They tell us who the Messiah is meant to be, and they tell us how human beings respond to even God's best.

When Jews heard Isaiah speak Chapter 9, or heard it read for seven centuries when they gathered to worship and pray, it is easy to imagine how their hopes soared.

> Unto to us a child is born,
> Unto us a son is given,
> And the government shall be upon his shoulder;
> And his name shall be called
> Wonderful,
> Counselor,
> Almighty God,
> The Everlasting Father,
> The Prince of Peace.
> Of the increase of his government and peace there shall be no end.   (Isaiah 9: 6-7, KJV)

Whatever the source of Israel's national humiliation, the promised Messiah was their hope. It may have been the latest version of the Philistines with yet another Goliath ready to do battle, or the Babylonians and Persians warring over Israel's spoils, or Greek armies rampaging across the land, or the Roman boot on their throat. With their own empire hopes in ruins, the glory days long gone, their beloved Temple desecrated and destroyed – it was time for another King David. Therein lies the problem. King David was all too human. Courageous, ferocious, victorious, yes. Also, adulterous and conniving. Brilliant and gifted. And so bloody that God denied him the privilege of building the first Temple. Yet, desperate times require desperate measures, and such measures open the way for unlikely leaders. Israel yearned for another King David.

Isaiah's Chapter 9 promised an extraordinary leader "upon the throne of David and upon his kingdom ... from henceforth and forevermore." They knew the powerful phrases: "wonderful, counselor, God, peace." But with your lands confiscated, your wealth stolen, your children exploited, your national identity in tatters, your existence mocked, and with the daily onslaught of rape and pillage at some enemy's hands, the individual Israeli's focus was probably on the words "almighty, everlasting, Prince." The promise of a renewed royalty sitting on David's throne, with both the fullness and "the increase" of that government assured, that was a Messiah worth following.

Later in Isaiah the bloom is off the rose of prophetic idealism. Isaiah 53 lays out the truth of how God's best are treated through the ages. In our time, Gandhi, Lincoln, Martin Luther King, Jr. are the obvious and tragic examples. Earlier I mentioned my favorite church in Bratislava, led by Franciscans, where, up near the altar, is the preserved corpse of Saint Reparatus. Reparatus was a young Roman soldier in the fourth century who chose to follow Christ. Like many before him, and many since, he was killed for living his faith. Faith-living seems always to threaten those whose profession is to threaten. The China of today, the USSR of the 20th Century, certain Islamic countries, right wing politics everywhere – why do they fear a wonderful counselor, a Prince of Peace? And why, as Isaiah predicted, will that special "child born, son given" end up like Saint Reparatus, Lincoln, King and so many more?

In startling fashion, Isaiah 53 describes the coming Messiah in a chapter often titled "The Suffering Servant". He will be "despised, rejected, a man of sorrows, acquainted with grief"; he will be thought of as repulsive, revolting, ugly, "no beauty or majesty to attract us to him." To the observer he will appear "stricken, smitten by God, afflicted." Does it get worse? Yes. Isaiah is just getting started on how those entrusted with God's saving mission can be expected to be welcomed.

> He was wounded for our transgressions,
> He was bruised for our iniquities;
> The chastisement of our peace was upon him;
> By his stripes we are healed ...
> The Lord has laid on him the iniquity of us all.
> He was oppressed and afflicted, yet he opened not his mouth;
> He is brought like a lamb to the slaughter.
>
> (Isaiah 53: 1-7)

All to good purpose, Isaiah assures us. Our salvation, our peace with God, our forgiveness is won by the sacrifice of one innocent man. My Jesus. The opposite of any generation's King David.

Two of my heroes were older English women missionaries whom I knew in the 1970s. They escaped a slaughter in old Zaire (the Congo), and then went back. When I asked them "why?" their answer was to quote this profound hymn.

My Jesus

> When I survey the wondrous cross
> on which the prince of glory died …
> love so amazing, so divine
> demands my love, my soul, my all.
> ("When I Survey the Wondrous Cross,"
> Isaac Watts, 1707)

Such understanding and gratitude are echoed in "How Great Thou Art," the second verse.

> And when I think that God,
> His Son not sparing,
> Sent him to die,
> I scarce can take it in.
> That on the Cross,
> My burden gladly bearing,
> He bled and died
> To take away my sin.
> Then sings my soul, my Savior God, to Thee
> How great Thou art,
> How great Thou art.
> ("How Great Thou Art," Stuart K. Hine, 1953)

Both hymns offer the two contrasting promises about the Messiah. The cross is wondrous, he is the Prince of Glory, his love is amazing and divine. And yet it is on that cross, bearing our burdens, that he bleeds and dies. "I scarce can take it in" gives way to exclaiming "How great Thou art."

This is the paradox of Jesus. Once upon a time, in O little town of Bethlehem, away in a manger, while shepherds watched their flocks by night, and angels from the realms of glory sang *Gloria in Excelsis Deo*, before

Jesus in the Bible

three kings of Orient followed the Star of Wonder, at that moment in Jewish history people were fervently waiting for a superhero Messiah. They would soon get, as we do, "the Suffering Servant." Yet we believe in, and await the fulfillment of, our Prince of Peace.

After that Silent Night, Holy Night, Jesus spends thirty-three years on earth, fully human. He talks, he does, he teaches, he shows, he berates, he heals, he dies as he lives, he lives some more, talking and doing and teaching some more. Then, as he promised, he's gone. It happened as quickly as I just wrote it.

After Jesus fulfilled his Messianic purpose, it was left to others to carry that purpose to the world: to make sense of Jesus for the world of every epoch.

Jesus left behind eleven proven, dedicated disciples. He also left an inner circle of maybe twenty, and a larger circle of another hundred. Scattered across Israel were more people who met him, heard him, were touched and/or inspired by him. Quite a few had their whole lives redirected by him. The ground was fertile for a movement.

The book of Acts includes a fascinating verse. The events of Jesus' Holy Week have him praised and adored, questioned and interrogated, betrayed and abandoned, arrested and tortured, denied and mocked and crucified. The Apostles' Creed puts it succinctly, "he was crucified, dead and buried." But not quite the end of the story.

Acts 1:3 picks up after the dead and buried part, taking us into Easter and beyond.

My Jesus

> He presented Himself alive after his suffering, by many convincing proofs, appearing to them over a period of forty days and speaking of the things concerning the Kingdom of God.

"Convincing proofs" plus my earlier mentioned "lives redirected by him" are part and parcel of the same thing. Together, they move us to faith, or we remain unmoved. There were the crowds who heard him preaching and teaching, remembering a parable or a beatitude or a new commandment. There was the multitude fed by a few loaves of bread and a couple of fish. A storm calmed. A dead daughter raised. A slave healed from a distance. Literal and figurative lepers welcomed and cleansed. His whole public life left people dazzled, puzzled and inspired. Jesus' daily life of miracles and wonders made the post-Easter "convincing proofs" more convincing. In my poem *Something Happened That Day* I consider the full range of events from Jesus' life that make us theologically fidget and spiritually wonder on the way to faith.

> Something happened that day
> some wondrous surprise
> that defies
> the explanation
> of mind or eyes
> something beyond belief
> but there it is
> to be believed
> Something happened that day
> some imagined possibility
> brought concrete reality to its knees

Jesus in the Bible

Something unknowable got known
something undoable got done
something peculiar
made folks remember
something "passing strange"
as they used to say
happened that day
Something outside the normal range
of whatever
human endeavor
finds acceptable.

Lazarus raised from the dead
thousands fed
with little fish
and too little bread ...
Something happened that day

Some spoken word
some inner thought
some outward touch
A leper made clean
A woman redeemed
Legion set free
A blind man could see
all would say
Something happened that day
something came their way
A whisper of the Spirit wind
A little miracle within

From birth in Bethlehem

to victory in Jerusalem
and everything in between
calming troubled waters on the sea
walking on water in Galilee
it cannot be explained away
Something happened that day

Nero's torches
Japanese crosses
Roman Coliseum
and tyrant's prison
tempted folks to weigh
carefully
whether something happened that day.

But something persevered
something rang true
something could not be denied
something that could not happen
happened some way that day
Something
took breath and doubt away.
Something
happened
that day.

(*Fieldstones of Faith,* Vol.2, David Johnson Rowe)

After the resurrection we get a good hint of these convincing proofs. He meets with discouraged followers who had fled, disconsolate, despite the rumors of his resurrection. With astounding grace, he forgave the broken Peter three times as an act of restoration. When

Jesus in the Bible

Thomas was overwhelmed by doubt, Jesus goaded him to faith. He fed the disciples, cooking breakfast for them. He sought people out, entertained questions. The forty days of convincing proofs culminated in a stirring final appearance, complete with the Great Commission marching orders, enduring promises, and his dramatic ascension. This left some people so convinced that they went on to confront the whole world with the Gospel. And it left some still doubting, with questions that persist to this very day. Jesus does that to people. His very proofs can be too challenging to believe. Believing in a physical presence hanging around after death can be easier than loving your enemy, blessing both peace-making and being persecuted, forgiving seventy times seven, or spending your life "doing unto the least of these."

What convinces some people of what is possible may also convince others of its *impossibility*. Both are movements with lasting power.

On Pentecost, seven weeks after the Easter resurrection, one movement blossomed. Filled with the very spirit that Jesus had promised them, those humble, unsophisticated, overwhelmed disciples spoke their faith so boldly that 3000 people decided to believe in Jesus as The Christ-Messiah, and to be baptized. Most amazingly, they decided to give up everything, join together, live together, all to better focus on this Jesus. (All references are to Acts 2).

Wrap your mind around that. A loose friendship group of 120 people is suddenly joined by three thousand

My Jesus

strangers who look to them for everything: breakfast, toilets, and Jesus.

Remember, at that moment they are all practicing, observant Jews, all 3,120 of them; they are all living together as a commune in Jerusalem. Necessity being the mother of invention, the disciples formed the first organizational principles of what would become Christianity. Those initial steps toward structure put them on the road to becoming a unique religion in their own right.

The structure was simple. The disciples would teach and pray. They were the spiritual elders, the first pastors. Then, among the other people, deacons were chosen to get the nitty-gritty done, looking after the basic needs of a rapidly expanding movement. Meanwhile, this new community of faith in Jesus willingly chose to share everything each one had. The overall guiding principle some people might attribute to Communism, but it's ours: "from each according to their ability, to each according to their need" (Acts 2: 44-5). Other than that, "they devoted themselves to the apostles' teaching and to fellowship, to the breaking of bread and to prayer ... filled with awe at the many signs and wonders ... and the Lord added to their number daily" (Acts 2: 42-47). That was the first church: being together, teaching, learning, praying, helping one another.

But what was taught? They were all Jews, sitting in the shadow of the most sacred Temple, and every day they gathered to be taught. Taught what?

Jesus in the Bible

There was no New Testament at that time, no four Gospels, no Paul's Epistles. There was no church or religion. No Apostles' Creed.

Instead, there was a select group of men and women who had been through thick and thin with Jesus for the better part of three years. They became the vast Oral Tradition on which Christianity is based. They were there. They had recollections, words, stories, teachings, memories. One person would say this, and trigger another to add that. Stories led to stories. This was a time in human history when Oral Tradition was vital and alive. People were attuned to hearing, accustomed to telling.

Those friends, followers, family and disciples were the original "Living Bible," the New Testament part. They taught the basics just as we would if we were introducing a new idea, project, concept, program or movement. Give some background, offer a few details, tell some stories, link it all to the punchline. For Jesus' followers, whatever they taught was only the lead-up to Good Friday and Easter, their punchline. That was the heartbeat of the Gospels: the depth of God's love shown by the sacrifice of our human Jesus on the cross, and shown by the victory of our divine Jesus through resurrection.

On the way to such a startling climax, those who had been with or near to the unfolding drama of Jesus' life would offer stories and quotes and memories, scenes from their own "Memory Palace" constructed room by room to hold precious recollections. This miracle and that parable, added to this encounter and that teaching were prelude to what made Jesus special: his willful death and absolute resurrection. In effect, they would tell how Jesus said such and such a wonderful thing, and how Jesus had done such and such a helpful thing. But nobody understood it, so he was killed. Yet God brought him back to life to prove to you and me that real life is through Jesus. That was the message.

Simple and effective, so people flocked to that early communitarian church. Quickly, however, persecution began. Authorities are always made nervous by the mere presence of upstarts with their own loyalties and understanding. The Jewish leaders ruling the Temple and the Roman leaders ruling the Jewish people could not have been happy with thousands of first century communitarian Christ-believers creating havoc all over downtown Jerusalem. That was disorderly conduct almost by definition and necessity, when above all Rome demanded order from the Jews. And Jewish leaders wanted order within Judaism. The Jesus movement disordered both. But the persecution that was meant to break up the movement instead spread it. Forced out of Jerusalem, little coffee klatches of Christ-believers were scattered across Israel, and then beyond, especially when Paul entered the picture with the unbridled fervor of a new convert. He devoted his life to circumambulating the whole area, first establishing churches (gatherings) and then nurturing churches with his epistles (letters). The story of Jesus soon reverberated down to Ethiopia, up to Greece, and on to Rome.

Each new place, each new convert, was a step farther and farther away from the uniform centrality of

Jerusalem and the Jerusalem-based disciples. It became more pressing to have a message, and to stay on message.

Perhaps that is when the "quest for the historical Jesus" truly began, almost at the start. Who was he? What do we know about him? What do people need to know? Or believe.

In Charlotte Allen's *The Human Christ,* Allen emphasizes the contrast between what was known and what was "Kerygma." Kerygma is the message, the proclamation, what needed to be preached.

From Day One of what would become Christianity, choices were made about what to tell, what to believe, what to include. Later that would lead to certain books making it into the Bible and others not, and to endless battles, often literally, about what is heresy and what is not. But in the early days it was more about what was essential and tactical. The Gospels of Luke and John state that clearly. Luke's Gospel begins with,

> Many have undertaken to draw up an account of the things that have been fulfilled among us, just as they were handed down to us by those who from the first were eyewitnesses and servants of the word. Therefore, since I myself have carefully investigated everything from the beginning, it seemed good also to me to write an orderly account (Luke 1:1-3) ... of all that Jesus began to do and to teach until the day he was taken up to heaven. (Acts 1:2).

And the Gospel of John concludes by admitting its selectivity:

My Jesus

> This is the disciple who testifies to these things and who wrote them down. We know that his testimony is true. Jesus did many other things as well. If every one of them were written down, I suppose that even the whole world would not have room for the books that would be written.
>
> (John 21: 24-25)

It's as if to say that there's more to Jesus than meets the eye or the pen. But here's what you need to know.

Having put down what we need to know, the next challenge was, and is, to discern what needs to be proclaimed. What is the Kerygma of the day, or the age?

That may explain why, when the Gospels tell us what they knew and experienced, the Gospels of Matthew and Luke give us the whole Christmas story, including the Virgin Birth. The writers knew it in the sense that they had heard it and believed. The Gospels of Mark and John don't include Christmas.

When early Christianity moved to the age of Kerygma, to the time of proclaiming the Gospel, the Christmas story was sidelined. It's not in the Acts, or the Epistles, or Revelation. That was a selective process, a choice of emphasis. In future generations the Virgin Birth makes a huge comeback, ending up in the Apostles' Creed as an essential belief. The 18th and 19th centuries resurrected Christmas to an almost unrecognizable but prominent degree.

In Chapter One we saw that the literary, artistic and theological quests for the most authentic Jesus changed from era to era. Likewise, the selection process for

Kerygma undergoes reformation and revision. New York Times columnist David Brooks imagined writing an end-of-decade column from the future, 2030, looking back on the decade of 2020-29. Nestled among political and economic prophecies, he suggests that the 2020s will enjoy a resurrection of faith among young adults. They will return to church in places that are energetic and charismatic in the broader sense, with ministries and beliefs that are pro-LGBTQ, pro-life, activist about climate change, and committed to animal rights (David Brooks, The New York Times, Jan.3, 2020). And my guess is, with some certainty, a zeal for racial healing and reconciliation.

That is new Kerygma, but it is still Kerygma. It is finding within the life and teachings of Jesus the stuff for today's Good News.

Those early first, second and third generation Christians also wrestled with Kerygma choices. What to preach? What to emphasize? Theirs was a Jesus who offered a new way of being: pure in heart, sacrificial, generous, loving to the extreme extreme, unworried, unburdened, bold with authorities, humble with humanity, confident with divinity. That was the Jesus of the Gospels not yet or just written but known by personal experience and trusted hearsay. On that they built a theological construct, dizzying and profound, needing to be proclaimed. It was quite a leap for those first Christ-followers, still observant Jews and steeped in groundbreaking monotheism, to offer Jesus as the Son of God.

My Jesus

Two sides of the same story equate to the two natures of Jesus, human and divine. There is that nature of Jesus to which we can aspire: Christlikeness. And that which is beyond us: Divinity, a place in the Trinity. There is nothing that Jesus told us to be that we cannot be. And what we cannot be, like atonement, he does for us.

As this thinking developed in inaugural Christianity, the result is that much of the New Testament is less a retelling of what Jesus said and did and more of an explanation of what Jesus means in the Big Picture.

This culminates in the exquisitely beautiful second chapter of Paul's letter to the Philippians. After emphasizing the suffering servant-likeness of Jesus, Paul concludes:

> Wherefore God hath exalted him
> and given him a name above
> every other name:
> that at the name of Jesus
> every knee shall bow
> of every living thing,
> and every tongue confess
> that Jesus Christ is Lord,
> to the Glory of God the Father.
> (Philippians 2: 8-11)

Not just Mr. Nice Guy. Or prophet, seer, philosopher, Rabbi, healer. Or even Holy Man. The Kerygma is no longer what Jesus said on a gently sloping mount, or who he healed while visiting a particular house, or how he handled a hungry crowd or a stormy lake or an angry mob. The Kerygma now is that Jesus is God made flesh,

Jesus in the Bible

dwelling among us, ushering in a new sense of the world called the Kingdom of God. The Kerygma now is about a power unleashed, a Holy Spirit indwelling, a path to life lived at such a level that eternity is continuation. And guaranteed.

Dare I summarize so far? The Jewish people taught that God would break through the torment of history to provide a Messiah so distinguishable that the world would acknowledge their rightness and righteousness as a people, a nation, and a religion. They, at last, would be a "light unto the Gentiles," just as promised to Abraham. The wait would be worth it.

With the winds of Easter triumph at their backs, Jesus' followers let loose a wave of faith that, if followed, could transform Israel, the Roman Empire, the world, and you yourself. The wait was worth it.

To conclude this chapter, I'll ask you to consider one improbable Kerygma that set Christianity on its singular path. Jesus' grandest expectations of us are enobling. Many spiritual heroes have urged us to be the best versions of ourselves we can accomplish. But Paul's Kerygma on the resurrection is astonishing. When we look for proof of the Holy Spirit's inspiration of scripture, this meets the standard.

1 Corinthians 15 is sandwiched between two entirely mundane matters: Keeping order in worship in Chapter 14, taking up offerings in Chapter 16. But in the middle Paul explains the unexplainable. Resurrection, eternal life, heaven, life after death, the relationship between the

My Jesus

miracle of Easter and the miracle awaiting us, Paul tackles it all.

Fifteen hundred times I have been with families after the death of a loved one. That is 1500 families whose hearts are aching, broken, who feel lost, abandoned, angry; whose hope and faith are teetering. It is also 1500 times when people are looking at me and begging me to get them through it. Some daring me to make sense of it all. My funerals have been for pre-birth and stillborn babies, infants, teenagers, murderers and murdered, suicides, overdoses, old age, centenarians. Sudden deaths, expected deaths, long overdue deaths. Church goers and church haters, from church-going families to church-hating families. From tragedy to blessing. Across that swath of sorrow, I am invited in, carrying the wisdom of Jesus and his believers. Through these years, I've found a bevy of scriptures, stories, poems that break the ice, touch a soul, heal a heart.

Nothing tops Paul when he likens death and resurrection to the whole cycle of farming. Even the most urban and urbane American likes to think they have roots in the soil. As a result, Paul's farmer analogy draws people to faith in the inexplicable resurrection.

Paul begins with a simple statement of Christian fact: "Christ died for our sins, he was buried, he was raised" (1 Corinthians 15: 3-4). That is early Christian Kerygma, on message to the "T." That worked in the early days, when a lot of people knew somebody who knew somebody who saw Jesus. But it wasn't long before Paul met resistance. This whole chapter is a fresh defense of resurrection

Jesus in the Bible

teaching. He admits there are doubters and deniers, building to an emotional admission:

> If the dead are not raised, then Christ has not been raised either. And if Christ has not been raised then your faith is futile, you are still in your sins. Then those who have died are lost ... and we are of all people most to be pitied.
>
> (1 Corinthians 15: 16-19)

But ...

One of our church members preached a summer sermon titled "But God," counting all the ways in which God interrupted impossible situations to accomplish the impossible. This "but" (verse 20) may be the biggest of all. "But Christ has indeed been raised from the dead, the first fruits of those who have fallen asleep." There is the introduction to farming, "first fruits." Jesus is the harbinger of God's great harvest, when the lives that have been ended and planted in the soil (burial, dust to dust, etc.), those earthy bodies will be transformed. Verses 35-49 remind us of the changing seasons, and what that life cycle seems and does. Fall comes, leaves change color and die, winter is bleak, trees and gardens are barren, life seems dreary. Then Spring comes. Planting season. Tiny seeds that bear no resemblance to the wheat or corn or vegetable or fruit that will soon be our bounty, they are planted with hope and expectation. Then we wait. And wait longer. But the appearance of the first fruits gives us every confidence of a complete harvest. And people get it. That is why I read this out loud:

> What you sow does not come to life unless it dies. When you sow, you do not plant that body that will be, but just a seed, perhaps of wheat or of something else. But God gives it a body as God has determined, and to each kind of seed God gives its own body ... There are heavenly bodies and there are earthly bodies; but the splendor of the heavenly bodies is one kind, and the splendor of the earthly bodies is another kind ... So it will be with the resurrection of the dead. The body that is sown is perishable, it is raised imperishable; it is sown in dishonor, it is raised in glory; it is sown in weakness, it is raised in power; it is sown a natural body, it is raised a spiritual body.
>
> (1 Corinthians 15: 36b-44)

That's good Kerygma. The church took a basic, faith-based fact from Jesus' life and turned it into a universal truth that the world hungers to know.

A closing caution: not all Kerygmas are created equal. Our same Saint Paul embraces authoritarian, "we know best" government in the face of all evidence to the contrary.

> Everyone must submit to the governing authorities for there is no authority except that which God has established. The authorities that exist have been established by God. Consequently, he who rebels against the authority is rebelling against what God has instituted ... for rulers hold no terror for those who do right ... he is God's servant to do you good. (Romans 13:1-4).

Jesus in the Bible

So much for our Revolutionary War heroes, Betsy Ross, the founding Fathers, and anyone else with the backbone for freedom.

Similarly, Jesus' affirmation of women, and Paul's own experiences of women in leadership don't prevent Paul from hiding behind the social customs of the day.

> Women should keep silent in the churches. They are not allowed to speak, but must be in submission, as the Law says. If they want to inquire about something, they should ask their own husband, at home; for it is disgraceful for a woman to speak in the church.
>
> (1 Corinthians 14: 33b-35)

"Kerygma from me, not Kerygma from the likes of thee," Paul is saying pointedly to half of humanity.

It is also Paul who provides the allegedly Christian bias against gay people. Regarding gay people, women or individual liberty, Paul seemingly creates Kerygma based on his own hang-ups or fears, not on anything Jesus said or did.

To the contrary, Jesus spent his entire career defying convention. He's not just silent about gay people. He actively engages, in a most positive way, with every outlier, with anyone ostracized by others: an enemy soldier, a woman from Samaria, a man so full of demons his nickname was Legion, the very religious hierarchy that sought his end, outright traitors to Israel, and any other outcast that others had deemed untouchable. Yet we are to believe Paul's Kerygma over Jesus' Kerygma? Paul, truly the main theological architect of New

My Jesus

Testament Christianity, with his church planting and letter writing, wants to take matters important to him beyond anything Jesus taught.

That can be tempting. The power of the pen or the pulpit can be fertile ground for one's own Kerygma. It is simpler and easier than rooting preaching, teaching and doing in our Jesus of scripture, the Gospel Jesus.

Thus, Jesus is next.

FOUR

Jesus' Kerygma

What did Jesus think? Of his life? His purpose? His meaning?

The Christian mantra, "What would Jesus do?" (WWJD) is based on what Jesus did and said. He said and did a lot in three years, but three years are not that long.

It strikes me that Jesus' message is a bit like mathematics. A math teacher does not give you every infinite example of addition, subtraction, division or multiplication. Instead, students are given some guiding principles, a few basic agreements, and off we go. I learned the times table early on and was told to apply that to multiplication the rest of my life. It worked.

Jesus works.

He set out guiding principles, the essentials from God's point of view, lived in real time in his life. He showed what works, and he did it with urgency. One major attribute of Jesus, the aspect that cultural references depict most accurately, is his passion for meeting each day head on. Musicals, plays, movies, books, art all show that intensity. There was not a thing he said or did that was not crucial. It is with this caveat that we seek Jesus' Kerygma. The plain truth is that Jesus was his own Kerygma. His life was the message.

My Jesus

I don't think Jesus would be much interested in endless debates about dogma or scriptures. We Christians have spent too much time turning the Bible into a battleground, and dogma into litmus tests for inclusion.

Jesus, the person, is our real story, not just Jesus as the storyteller. Christianity has often turned faith into a thing. A certain dogma, a set creed, right politics or policies, a particular building; even the Bible has been so elevated that there is a word for it: Bibliolatry. Making the Bible into an idol, a thing to be worshipped.

Jesus doesn't get caught up in such debates. When John the Baptist was in prison, soon to be beheaded, he sent his own disciples to Jesus to ask point-blank, "are you the One? Or should we look for another?" (Matthew 11:3). John wanted to be sure that he had backed the right horse. He'd spent his life on a single purpose: "to prepare the way of the Lord." John's work was yet another fulfillment of Biblical prophecy about the Messiah: that somebody would prepare the way (Matthew 3:1-3). John had done his work faithfully. Now he wanted to know if Jesus was properly the right one for whom he had prepared the way and given his life.

Jesus' answer was, "Go back and report what I do and say: The blind receive sight, the lame walk, lepers are cleansed, the deaf hear, the dead are raised, and the good news is proclaimed to the poor" (Matthew 11:4-5). Notice that he didn't respond, "I was born in Bethlehem. My mother was a Virgin. I'll soon ride into Jerusalem on a donkey. I'm checking all the boxes. What more do you want?"

That is surface stuff. It is good to know that he fulfilled prophecy. Biography, facts and figures, can be affirming and confirming. But they are not the substance of Jesus.

It is fair to ask, then, what is the substance you must know? I use "must" in the way we often do when hyping something we really like, that works for us. We talk it up, telling friends and strangers, "You must read this book ... you must visit Bratislava ... you must eat at Toscano's in Cambridge ... you must ski the Rockies!" We are convinced, so we want to share our conviction.

You may not like religious doorbell ringers, but you can admire those Mormons and Jehovah's Witnesses who are so convinced of their faith that they simply cannot sit at home and keep it to themselves. Young Mormons leave college in their late teens to give two years to the "must" sharing of the unique Mormon take on Christianity. You can find them in American suburbs far from Utah in every respect, or the far reaches of the earth, very much living the contradictory idealism of the Broadway musical *The Book of Mormon*.

By the way, if I may? The best public relations decision the Mormons made, in the face of that very satirical ribald musical, was that they chose not to urge a boycott but instead launched an ad campaign all over New York City: "Seen the Musical? Now Read the Book."

My Jesus

My approach is similar but in reverse. People think they know "The Good Book" well enough. But I'm saying: "Read the Book? Now See Jesus."

Jesus' three years of saying and doing run the gamut of life, providing a vast range of "must see" scriptures.

At weddings I tell the story of Jesus at a wedding in Cana, the occasion of his first miracle. It is a small-town wedding for a local family; it's a big deal, with everyone invited including Jesus and the Disciples. When the wedding reception runs out of wine, Jesus' mother strongly implies that he must fix the problem. That's when Jesus turns the water into wine (John 2:1-11). The point is that Jesus is never confined by anyone's sense about what's doable, what's important, what's a priority. My takeaway from Jesus saving the wedding party from embarrassment is this: that if it is important to you, it is important to God. Jesus' life showed that nothing is beneath or beyond God's interest.

This is his Kerygma. He turns water into wine. Heals a young boy of apparent epilepsy. Feeds a hungry crowd that could just as reasonably been sent home. Challenges tradition. Breaks tradition. Starts tradition. Takes accepted law (thou shalt not kill or commit adultery) and goes deeper (don't get angry, don't lust). Helps a woman with out-of-control bleeding. Gives great object lessons using a fig tree, the tables of moneychangers, and a Roman coin. Writes in the dirt while saving an adulterous woman from stoning. Spits on a blind man's eyes. Gets down on his knees to wash the Disciples' feet. Meets with the enemy. Dines with traitors. Tells stories. Walks on water. Calms storms. Stirs up his hometown synagogue. Turns a hated Samaritan into a hero. Tells the Disciples to arm. And disarm. Redefines the Sabbath. Redefines leadership. Redefines giving. Redefines sacrifice.

Redefines God.

All of this is "must see" Jesus.

To prime your pump for selecting key pieces of Jesus' Kerygma, consider these four musts.

The Sermon on the Mount, Matthew 5-7

This sermon is the longest teaching of Jesus we have, and it is head-spinning. If you want an inside look at Jesus on the broadest array of topics, these chapters give it. It is almost insulting to merely list the Sermon on the Mount as a small paragraph in a larger chapter which is only part of a book. When Alida and I saw Michelangelo's David in Florence, and Winged Victory at the Louvre, and George Inness' paintings at the Clark, our immediate thought was, why go on? Why not stay here with this? What more could possibly be gained? Likewise with the Sermon on the Mount. Know the Sermon on the Mount, know Jesus.

Watch him describe the path to true happiness in the Beatitudes (Matthew 5:1-12). Hear him put flesh and bones on old laws so that they take on deeper meaning (vs. 17-42). Be inspired to be "salt of the earth" and "light of the world" (vs. 13-16). Imagine being the kind of person to turn the other cheek, go the extra mile, love and pray for your enemies, give and forgive. Aim for perfection (vs. 38-48). Learn to pray (Matthew 6: 5-15). Get your priorities straight (vs. 19-34). Stop judging and worrying. Become bold in faith (Matthew 7: 7-12). See the Golden Rule laid out before you. Bear fruit (vs. 15-20). Build strong (24-27).

All that in one sermon. It really is Winged Victory. You don't need to stand in line for the Mona Lisa.

John 3:16

Long ago it was called "The Gospel in a Nutshell." It almost doesn't need to be spoken, just referenced. Beginning in the 1970s a fellow named Rollen Stewart kept showing up at major sporting events wearing a giant, rainbow-colored afro wig. At key moments he'd stand up, holding a simple sign: John 3:16.

There he was at the Super Bowl, at the World Series, live at the US Open. For many, the reference said it all. Others scurried to dust-covered Bibles to look it up. Football star quarterback Tim Tebow often had "John 3:16" imbedded in the eye black he wore during games. "For God so loved the world that he gave his only begotten son, that whosoever believeth in him shall not perish but have everlasting life." God's love, Jesus' purpose, and our benefit are neatly summarized in twenty-five words.

The founder of my New England prep school was D.L Moody, America's foremost evangelist of the 19th century. During a long crusade, Moody was unexpectedly called away, and the elders designated a young preacher to step in for a night or two.

He strode to the pulpit and announced that he would be preaching on the most important verse of the Bible, John 3:16. He read it, and then preached on it.

The next night he made the same announcement and preached a second sermon on John 3:16. Moody continued to be delayed and, night after night, the young preacher surprised everyone by summoning a new sermon from the same verse.

After a week's absence, Moody returned. Hearing of the young preacher's ability, he asked him to preach that night as well. And once again, he introduced John 3:16 as the most important verse in the Bible, read it aloud, and, yet again, found new riches to mine in that "Gospel in a Nutshell." So it is. God's love, Jesus' purpose, and our benefit neatly summarized in twenty-five words.

John 1:1-14: The Incarnation

To be The Christ is, by definition, to be set apart. Christ means "the anointed," someone picked out by God to do a job only he must do. Christ is not Jesus' last name; it is a descriptive and honorific title earned by his life's work. He proved himself to be the Christ. He wasn't the Christ until he lived it.

There are other singularities to Jesus, from Virgin Birth to Resurrection, with a number of supernatural triumphs in between that are certainly singular. Walking on water, raising Lazarus from the dead, healing long distance by merely his say-so come to mind.

My Jesus

The undergirding of it all is the Incarnation. From the Latin, "Incarnation" means to embody, to become meat (carne), to put flesh in the game (in-carne). Theologically, the Incarnation is God's decision to become one of us, flesh and bone, living a human and earthly life. St. Paul puts it directly:

> Jesus thought it not robbery to be equal with God. But made himself of no reputation and took upon himself the form of a servant and made in the likeness of men...he humbled himself and became obedient unto death on the cross.
>
> (Philippians 2:6-8)

This is stunning stuff. Knowing full well that he is God, personally integral to the whole God-head idea, Jesus willingly drops way down more than a peg or two. All the way to the likes of us. Most telling are the phrases that he "made himself of no reputation...took upon himself the form of a servant...humbled himself." In other words, Jesus took Incarnation seriously. Very intentionally, he chose a life begun in poverty and oppression, experienced terror and persecution, felt loss and betrayal, knew pain on every level. Even death. That's human.

John is more poetic, providing a parallel to the more famous Christmas stories of Matthew and Luke.

> In the beginning was the Word,
> And the Word was with God,
> And the Word was God.
> He was in the beginning with God.
> All things were made through Him,

> And without Him nothing was made that was made.
> In Him was Life,
> And the life was the light of all people.
> And the Word became flesh
> And dwelt among us,
> And we beheld His glory,
> The glory as of the only begotten of the Father.
>
> (John 1:1-3, 14)

Pure Incarnation. God as Word. God as flesh. God as Trinity. The Word, sent by God's love, became flesh and "we beheld him, "John writes. They saw it all at work. The blood that ran through Jesus' veins was the same life force that created the universe. There is no disunity among the Trinity. They are one. For the duration of Jesus' short life, we had the benefit of God with us, God like us, God one of us. At last, we are truly known.

The Cross and Resurrection

I've lived long enough to see the Resurrection easily denied, easily explained away, easily minimized. It becomes a sweet allegory of spring, a lovely symbol of rebirth after the harsh reality of winter. I've done it myself. Searching to explain Christian bodily resurrection to an Easter congregation of sophisticated New Yorkers, I happened across the news story of a supermarket opening in Harlem, a sure sign of rebirth, back in the day. The point? If a grocery store can reopen in Harlem, anything can happen. That was my Easter story.

My Jesus

In the years since, I've lurched between thinking that analogy was silly or profound. Mostly, it seemed silly.

Yet in a conversation with my mentor, Tomáš Halík, he emphasized the need for more resurrections, for resurrections of every kind to be noted all around us. Each resurrection links us to Easter's eternal truth, that with God the end is not the end.

Meanwhile, the Cross is rejected in some circles. If God is "Our Father who art in heaven" and Jesus is "his only begotten son," then the idea of God the Father forcing Jesus the Son to an excruciating death on the cross is child abuse. That may be a contemporary sensibility forced upon an ancient theology of atonement, but sensibility does that. Furthermore, the old idea of God needing blood sacrifice in order to forgive humankind, to look kindly on humankind, is unseemly, even in retrospect. Believers are seemingly caught between the unbelievable (Resurrection) and the unacceptable (Cross). It can be a tight squeeze.

For me, the Cross makes sense. In the United States, and surely most countries, we revere those who give their lives for others: Soldiers, Fire and Police First Responders. Into battle, into a burning house, into an active crime scene, these men and women are prized and treasured; more so if they "make the ultimate sacrifice", death. We especially honor those who do so knowingly and voluntarily. Andrew Carnegie established a fund that awards grants to those who are not in professions that require life or death action, and yet put their lives on the line to save others. Into rushing rivers, crushed cars and

Jesus' Kerygma

workplace accidents, our everyday heroes show us that we are all capable of more love and compassion than thought possible. Jesus always thought the possible, without limit.

Jesus' self-sacrifice on the cross is many things, but not surprising. It both makes sense and speaks volumes. It is Jesus' Kerygma.

And so is the resurrection. Both are loud and clear proclamations, symbolically and literally. Symbols can be powerful without being literal. Understanding Jesus' death on the cross as a gift of love, and the resurrection as an affirmation of life, is an easy lesson to teach and preach. However, to imagine a beaten, tortured, horrifically executed man returning to the fullness of life as a living presence is rooted in faith, above all. It is more than a supermarket opening, however vital and optimistic.

I cannot explain the resurrection. Attempts to use science to prove faith help neither. An old Christian film, wanting to show that science and faith could co-exist, took the fact that everything is made of moving molecules to "prove" that it was scientifically, mathematically possible for the moving molecules of the resurrected Jesus to perfectly align with the spaces between moving molecules of a locked door. Ergo, the fact that Jesus showed up after his death and burial and entered through a closed door to meet the disciples proves the Resurrection.

Not for me. What proves the resurrection for me is, first and foremost, that that first generation of believers

My Jesus

was so thoroughly convinced that nothing could shake their faith. Martyrdom beckoned each one in gruesome ways. This carried on for centuries, most often accompanied by an out: Recant your faith, deny the resurrection, turn your back on Jesus and live. Yet, one after another made a choice to die rather than reject Jesus' most outrageous doings. Their experience of the living Christ, whether in person or in the heart, made it impossible to reject. His resurrection was that real.

I'm also convinced by people I trust who have never steered me wrong on anything. Their advice, counsel, wisdom, tips, guidance, Biblical reproof and correction, were each time on time and right. Why discount them when they assure me that Jesus was and is alive and well? A friend, Henry Mitchell, told me that if you have to choose between what your Mama told you and what the world told you, always go with your Mama. I broaden that to the faith of those close to me versus a world of popular doubt and impressive skeptics. I'm going with Mama, and those whose spiritual nurturing have a mother's touch. I believe in the Cross and the Resurrection.

Bishop T.D. Jakes, the media megastar of Christianity, once preached about Moses and the Burning Bush. In the scripture story God uses the Burning Bush to get Moses' attention, and then gives Moses the privilege of liberating the Israelites from slavery in Egypt. Jakes said most people focus on the Burning Bush rather than the message of liberation. True.

Christian believers and their disbelievers do the same. Getting caught up in doctrines and creeds and stumbling blocks, the message may be missed. Long before the internet, in the golden age of TV and Hollywood, Marshall McLuhan stated "the medium is the message." True enough. Jesus is the medium. Jesus is the message. Jesus is the Kerygma.

FIVE

Jesus Teaches Me a Thing or Two

I had a Baptist's baptism, a Congregational confirmation, a classic Catholic Baltimore Catechism training, a Christian prep school's mandatory Bible classes, college Philosophy and Religion core courses, a St. Paul lightning bolt conversion, and a solid seminary education.

Then God got to work on me. Eventually, all the pieces fit together. From childhood flannelgraph Bible stories to kissing the feet of Jesus in a Prague chapel dedicated to martyred priests, from Christian summer camp as a shocked kid to Christian boot camp every time I stepped out of my front door, God pounded home a message about Jesus.

"Look up," my father always told me, about most everything in life. Tough times, athletic pursuits, personal troubles, goals, challenges and obstacles, church work, family life, raising kids. "Look up," see the possibilities, hear the call, follow the progress. Eventually, all that looking up and around became my essential Jesus.

My first looking up was Acts 16:31; it was also my first wakeup call that there was more to Jesus than the flannelgraph stories told in the happy Sunday School classrooms of my childhood.

Jesus Teaches Me a Thing or Two

Acts 16:31 is my "salvation verse." What's a "salvation verse"? Let me explain.

At age eight my parents sent me away to summer camp. There's that phrase again, sent away, and this was definitely more the reform school version than my forested Northfield Mt. Hermon prep school.

I was eight, from Queens, where the Asphalt Jungle was my paradise. And now it's summer. As the classic rock song declared, "No more rulers, no more books, no more teacher's dirty looks ... School's out for the summer." What promise each day held. The cops let us open up the fire hydrants. Endless sandlot baseball games. Subway rides to Rockaway Beach. Jahn's Ice Cream Parlor.

Then, one day, I'm driven to the old Port Authority Bus Terminal in Times Square, the true bowels of the city. Stuffed in a bus, I get dropped six hours later in the Adirondack Mountains.

I was ushered to a cabin (what's that?), met bunkmates (what's that?), saw the communal latrine (what's that?), and it only got worse. First stop, aquatics (what's that?). My idea of swimming was best friends rumbling in the waves at Coney Island with no adult supervision. At Camp Hell, aquatics had rules, easily summarized: No. Whatever an eight-year-old would want to do in water, the answer was no. Then archery. Then horses. Could a day get any worse?

Word of Life, the camp was called, from a Bible verse, Philippians 2:16. In that verse, Paul tells his readers to "hold forth the word of life," meaning to hold fast, hold

My Jesus

firmly, hang on to the word of life he had been preaching. In a word, Jesus. Whatever concerns there are about some of Paul's ideas, he was pro-Jesus, as was the camp.

Word of Life Camp was there to get youngsters to know Jesus and then to "hold fast" to Jesus as they headed back to school, life, teenagerhood, or, for me, the streets I missed terribly.

Sarcasm aside, camp was okay. I never got over my fear of horses, or my dislike of archery, aquatics, lanyards, bugle calls, latrines, or bugs.

But the people were good, and "the word of life" was real. Everything built, as most summer camp experiences do, to a climax. Sacred or secular, Word of Life or Boy Scout Camp, Wilderness or Urban Plunge, bonding is the closing purpose. Bonfires, music, storytelling, recognition, farewells leave the camper believing they had found something, and wanting more. At Word of Life, we were bonded with Jesus.

Our penultimate night was dedicated to helping us find our "salvation verse," a verse just for you to carry with you the rest of your life. Gently guided by nice college kids who knew more Bible than we did, we newbies to camp and to Jesus were asked to find a verse. Not just any verse. It had to speak to one's own salvation. It had to carry that "Blessed Assurance, Jesus is Mine" feel. At age eight, they assured me my life ahead would be full of temptation, trial, testing, evil of every sort, the Devil ready to undo everything camp had done. I needed a verse to claim as my own, a Biblical mantra, a

Jesus Teaches Me a Thing or Two

confidence builder, a cross-shaped word amulet to ward off evil.

I found it. Acts 16:31. "Believe on the Lord Jesus Christ, and thou shalt be saved; and thy house". Which, they assured me, meant "household," your people.

Brief background. My "salvation verse" is the result of a dramatic prison escape. Paul and Silas were imprisoned for disturbing the peace and disrupting some shady, exploitive businessmen. An earthquake shook open the prison door. The chief jailer assumed they had escaped and knew he would be held accountable, so he prepared to take his own life. When Paul surprisingly intervened, the impressed jailer asked, "What must I do to be saved?" My "salvation verse" was Paul's answer.

As Christians we learn in stages. St. Paul was right when he wrote, "when I was a child I understood as a child … (then) I put childhood behind me. Now I know in part; then I shall know fully" (1 Corinthians 13:11-12). My grandfather began each day reading the Bible for three hours, because every few years he saw something new in verses he had read a thousand times.

My salvation verse was an early-stage learning. It started out just as Word of Life Camp hoped. There it was in black and white, in my Holy Bible, said by the Apostle Paul himself. Believe in Jesus and you're saved. Plus, it will be good for my family somehow. A childhood understanding.

Over time the "household" got bigger. Salvation got bigger. The focus got bigger than me. Jesus pushes us outward all the time. Our salvation, yours and mine,

My Jesus

impacts households and families in the broadest sense. Indeed, if salvation is only about me it gets turned into the height of selfishness. But Jesus pushes us beyond every boundary to the point where Paul is forced to declare what I never tire of repeating, "in Christ there is neither Jew nor Greek, male nor female, slave nor free. But all are one in Christ" (Galatians 3:28). The selfless life of Jesus overcomes any self-centered obsession, expanding our household. That must have been a tough message to preach when Paul wrote it to the Galatians around the year 50. Try preaching it today. Half the congregations in half the churches in America would walk out halfway through the sermon, and half the preachers would get fired. At a time of rising nationalism, entrenched borders, calls for walls, and anti-immigration fever; a time when gender fluidity is recognized more than ever before; a time when the Civil War gets refought daily over Confederate statues and flags, reparations, and southern plantation tours – at such a time we hear that Jesus is the architect behind a world without borders, gender, or race.

Paul's expansiveness echoes Jesus. Jesus was resoundingly firm that the Kerygma of his life was universal. In Matthew 28:19, and again in Acts 1:8, Jesus' final interactions are blunt: "go ye into all the world ... be my witness in Jerusalem, Judea, Samaria, to the ends of the earth." No boundaries.

My Acts 16:31 salvation verse had already pushed my faith outside of myself, tying it directly to my household. The rest of Jesus expands the idea of household to the universe. When church children sing "He's got the whole world in His hands, He's got the whole wide world in His hands" they are singing the Kerygma of Jesus. And when Jesus made a much-hated Samaritan the hero of his parable designed to explain "who is my neighbor?", that is his Kerygma.

This gets lived out most obviously in Jesus' healings. I am a firm believer that Jesus' healings were less about showing his power and more about driving home a Universal Truth, maybe with all capitals. Jesus does two things at once. He responds to the individual, one on one. It is said of certain people, "they feel your pain ... when they talk to you it is like you are the only person in the room". That is focus, and Jesus had it.

At the same time, he took that one-on-one and makes us think wider, way wider. Jesus' dealings with lepers and bleeding women, blind beggars and demon-filled outcasts, Roman Centurion and the corrupt Zacchaeus hiding in a tree force us to do the same. Look up, look around just as he did. Notice and ask. Who is in the tree, hiding? Who revolts you? Who gets shunned? Ignored? Who can't you stand the thought of? Who makes you feel icky, queasy, angry? And what the heck was Jesus doing with them?

In our Confirmation Class curriculum, one evening is devoted to "Who did Jesus Hang With?" It is a surprising list, just as it was for the people of Jesus' time. It shocked folks to see Jesus breaking bread with "publicans and sinners" (Mark 2:14-17). Nobody should have been surprised. Following in the radical footsteps of his cousin, John the Baptist, with the Baptist's own stamp of approval on him, Jesus' path was pretty clear. Cutting his teeth by preaching in his own hometown, reading aloud one of the most spiritually revolutionary verses in the Bible about advancing justice in every conceivable way (Luke 4:16-21), Jesus' handwriting was on the wall. His presence declared that things are going to be different. Religion won't be the same. Get used to it. In short order, Jesus is on a first-name basis with demons, with unclean and needy riffraff of every type, with the ruling class and the working class, with the religious elite and the truly downtrodden. Jesus hung with everyone willing to be hung with.

What a friend we have in Jesus? What a friend we are in Jesus? Yes, and yes, if our friends include the hungry, naked, imprisoned, thirsty, the least of these, the meek, persecuted, mournful. And anyone else defined as your household and not in your household. That doesn't leave anyone out, does it?

Yes, a "salvation verse" I found around a bonfire in the wilds of the Adirondacks at age eight has stuck with me. Enough so that, although I am a very minor author, when I autograph my books, I often affix Acts 16:31. As with the rainbow-haired John 3:16 sign-bearer, maybe my reference causes a few to look it up.

As life went on, other verses spoke to me more specifically. Life, with all its stages, requires verses with all their nuances. Being forgiven as I forgive others means little as a youngster. It takes on greater significance as my need for forgiveness and occasions to forgive multiply and intensify. Forgiveness, second chances, spiritual mulligans, do-overs seem both urgent and miraculous the more failures, mistakes, errors and sins I perpetrate.

I've only played golf once in my life, so I began and ended my golf career as a hacker. On the third hole I hit another laughably horrible shot, and, with one voice, my golf mates shouted "mulligan". I had never heard that word. To my amazement it meant that my ridiculous excuse for a shot did not count, would not be held against me, no penalty, no need to hunt for the ball in the woods. I was allowed to take a fresh swing, perhaps learning a thing or two from my mistaken first swing.

What a sport! I had spent my youth in the harsh world of baseball. Three strikes and you're out. Go to the bench. Sit down in abject humiliation. Endure the mockery of other teams, the disappointment of your team, the tough love of your coach, the silence or derision of the fans in the stands. Never was I told by the umpire or the opposing pitcher to forget it, come back, try again, you can do better.

Maybe Jesus was a golfer, with a built-in sense of how hard life can be, how easy it is to mess up, how beautiful it is to start with a clean slate.

In large part Jesus made his name by forgiveness. It is inexorably linked with his life. It is at the heart of his Lord's Prayer. When he saved an adulterous woman from being stoned to death by self-righteous men, his farewell to her was "go and sin no more" (John 8:11). When friends laid a paralytic at his feet, who had not had much chance to sin, Jesus startled everyone by first forgiving

My Jesus

him and then healing him. His critics snarked, "who the heck are you to forgive sins?", entirely missing the point and the person of Jesus (Mark 2:5-7). His openness to corrupt and oppressive sinners (Matthew the Tax Collector, the Roman Centurion, Nicodemus the Pharisee, Zacchaeus the cheat, the thief executed with him) is clearly forgiveness-based. Almost without words he is showing, "I see you as you are now, with me. I don't see you as you used to be."

My golfing mulligan-givers were doing the same. As awful as they knew me to be they were saying, "we know you're better than that". I've lost track of how many times God has said and done the same for me.

Jesus is defined, in part, by what others have said about him, what He said about Himself, and what we do with Him.

Much is open to interpretation. As a twelve-year-old Jesus startled his parents by getting separated during their family journey to Jerusalem. After three days of sheer panic, they find Jesus in the Temple "listening and asking questions" with the leading religious scholars of the day. If that wasn't shocking enough, when Mary and Joseph gently chided him Jesus' response was, "Didn't you know I had to be in my Father's House?" (Luke 2:41-52). The King James Version translates Jesus words as "I must be about my Father's business". Was Jesus, at age twelve, connecting the Trinitarian dots between himself as God the Son to God the Father? Or was he using Father in the same way he tells us to call God "Father" in our prayers? Both, perhaps.

Jesus Teaches Me a Thing or Two

Two scenes from the end of his life are quite telling. After another unpleasant encounter with critics, Jesus asked his disciples point blank a two-pronged question. "Who do men say that I am?" And in a follow up, "Who do you say that I am?" The disciples, like people today, like the questers of the earlier chapter, responded with some of the educated guesses doing the rounds before Simon Peter breaks through with the foundational answer of Christianity ever since, "Thou art the Christ, the Son of the Living God" (Matthew 16:13-16).

Jesus' response could not be clearer: "My Father in heaven revealed that to you. And on that Rock/Petra/Peter faith I will build my church" (Matthew 16:16-18). Protestants and Catholics diverge on this, as to whether the Church would be built on the person of Peter or on the faith expressed by Peter. Either way, Jesus is admitting that Peter is correct, word for word. He is the Christ, the Son of the Living God.

In stark contrast, in his final hours a beaten, tortured, about to be executed Jesus is brought before a tormenting crowd by Pontius Pilate. Dismissively, mockingly, Pilate says "Ecce homo" (John 19:5). Behold the man. The taunt is clear and pointed, as if to say to every Jew in Israel, you want a Messiah, you think God is sending you a savior? Remember all those "hail King David" palm-waving chants last Sunday? Well, here he is. Ecce homo. Behold the man.

Little did Pilate know how right he was. That was our Savior. Everything Isaiah promised. Everything Jesus promised. A bloody mess.

My Jesus

The Christianity of my lifetime has always lurched between two images, summarized best by the crucifix vs. the empty cross. The crucified Christ, hanging on a cross, his agony vividly portrayed by every inch of his body, blood pouring down from his thorn-encrusted brow and speared side and nailed hands and feet. Or his lifeless body slumping in surrender. It is finished.

However, in many churches the cross is empty, beautiful, crafted and gold-plated, polished and triumphant. That instrument of torture could not contain him, physically or spiritually. It is transformed into jewelry, a symbol of God's love, and victory.

The contrast is played out in old-timey hymns, none more clearly than "Alas, and did my Savior bleed?" The verses are mournful, apologetic.

> Alas, and did my Savior bleed?
> And did my Sovereign die?
> Would He devote that sacred head
> For such a worm as I?
>
> ("Alas, and Did My Savior Bleed?"
> Isaac Watts, 1707)

All five verses go on in that same confessional, guilt-ridden vein. Yet each verse is followed by a jaunty, peppy exultation:

> At the cross, at the cross
> Where I first saw the light
> And the burden of my heart rolled away
> It was there by faith
> I received my sight

And now I am happy all the day!"

The worm that made the Savior bleed is now happy all the day.

Half of Christianity dwells on the worm angle; the other half revels in being happy all the day. Both are expressing the reality of Jesus.

SIX

Jesus Doesn't Want Me For a Sunbeam

Kurt Cobain brought fleeting fame to an anti-sunbeam song on his "MTV Unplugged" concert, doing a cover of the Vaselines' original. The Vaselines' song is a jaded reproach to the sweet joy of a century-old favorite among Sunday School children.

Check them out:

>Jesus <u>doesn't</u> want me for a sunbeam
>'Cause sunbeams are not made like me
>And don't expect me to cry
>For all the reasons you had to die
>Don't ever ask your love of me
>Don't expect me to lie
>Don't expect me to cry
>Don't expect me to die for thee (or me?)
>   (The Vaselines, Eugene Kelly Frances McKee)

Or...

>Jesus wants me for a sunbeam
>To shine for Him each day
>In every way try to please Him
>At home, at school, at play.
>A Sunbeam, a sunbeam
>Jesus wants me for a sunbeam
>A sunbeam, a sunbeam
>I'll be a sunbeam for Him
>Jesus wants me to be loving,
>And kind to all I see

Jesus Doesn't Want Me For a Sunbeam

Showing how pleasant and happy
His little one can be
I will ask Jesus to help me
To keep my heart from sin
Ever reflecting his goodness
And always shine for Him
I'll be a sunbeam for Jesus
I can if I but try
Serving Him moment by moment
Then live with Him on high.

(Nellie Talbot, 1905)

Graffiti.

In all its spray can, faux vandalism, retro glory there it is: "Jesus Doesn't Want Me for a Sunbeam." WOW! There's a shocker. "Jesus <u>Wants</u> Me for a Sunbeam" is as bright and cheery and affirming a song as the title suggests. I've sung it hundreds of times, and taught it at Sunday Schools, Vacation Bible Schools and Christian summer camps. It seems perfectly clear. Jesus wants me, and you, to be one of his sunbeams, with all that implies.

Yet in Krakow, Poland we stumbled across this anti-sunbeam graffiti on a wall. Jesus most assuredly does not want you to be a sunbeam, the Krakow would-be Banksy declares.

Why not?

Is it anti-sunbeam, anti-Jesus, or anti-something else? What's the hang-up?

For context, Krakow was home to one of Hitler's notorious ghettoes, a way station before annihilation. Its citizens were imprisoned and killed, sooner or later. Former neighbors were no doubt employed or complicit in the whole embodiment of evil. Nobody was unscathed by the Holocaust horror.

There are no bystanders when it comes to great evil. We too often do it, allow it, vote it, help it, remain silent about it. That is true now, it was true then.

Just prior to the provocative sunbeam graffiti, Alida and I had toured Schindler's factory, made famous by Steven Spielberg's film about Schindler and his effort to save Jews. The factory is now a terribly moving museum of the Nazi era in Krakow, 1939-1945. Shaken and disturbed, we were walking toward the remnants of the ghetto wall the Jews were forced to build to imprison themselves behind. The wall was built of ten-foot-tall concrete slab facsimiles of Jewish cemetery headstones. The imagery was lost on no one.

On the way we walked through a Holocaust Memorial, a host of bronzed kitchen chairs scattered across a typical European cobblestone square. The chairs are meant to recall the chaos of Jews and other Poles uprooted and resettled, taking what they could in battered suitcases, with everyday life, like kitchen chairs, left behind.

And so, from the Nazi remembrances of Schindler's factory, after the memorial chairs and before the Jewish headstone ghetto walls, there is the graffiti: Jesus Doesn't Want You for a Sunbeam.

We allowed ourselves to wonder, what would lead to such a cynical declaration? What led Kurt Cobain to feature this song in his legendary MTV Unplugged concert? What led the Vaselines to write and sing it in the first place? We pulled up the song on my phone and listened to it carefully, still mystified, but able to hear the dismissive rejection of a particular, soothing Jesus. Don't need it. Don't want it. Won't be it.

You may have noticed the many faces of Buddha portrayed on statues, wall hangings, art. There is a contemplative Buddha, a teaching Buddha, a serene Buddha, a happy Buddha, a reclining Buddha, a laughing roly-poly Buddha. There are plenty of Jesuses, too, and the graffiti artist had one in mind. Don't give me that sunbeamy Jesus, the artist was saying.

I wanted to ask him or her about it, or Cobain, or the Vaselines. There's only a narrow segment of the population who grew up singing "Jesus wants me for a sunbeam," and you'd have to know it to turn against it. All three would have put some thought into this.

The pro-sunbeam crowd wants us to shine for Jesus, at home and school and play, to be loving, kind, pleasant, reflecting his goodness and avoiding sin. It is a rejection of all things evil, even the Holocaust.

The anti-sunbeam crowd is more fed up with the veneer of goodness, more jaded about humans. We're not made of sunbeam material, the song declares. Furthermore, don't blame me for whatever happens to whomever, including Jesus. And don't expect any heroics from me, either. It's a shoulder-shrug to evil, even the Holocaust.

Was the singer-songwriter saying that Jesus wouldn't want any part of what you are up to, or I'm up to, or the world is up to? Stationed in the middle of Holocaust Alley, such as it was in Krakow, with Auschwitz-Birkenau hovering nearby now as it did then, was it a commentary on any search for meaning, redemption, good that would dare suggest itself? Was it a direct slap at crass Christian evangelists who might capitalize on the Holocaust, offering platitudes caked in sugar while targeting Jews more subtly than yesteryear's opportunists? Or was the singer-songwriter saying, don't expect me to take on any Jesus-type heroics for the messes that humans create? "I'm not dying for thee," the song proclaims, with surprising King James English.

Cobain can't tell us what he meant. His suicide cut short life, career, thoughts, all that he might have become. Just like six million neighbors of the graffiti and Schindler and chairs.

But Cobain is not alone in rejecting one kind of Jesus or another. "I don't want your Jesus," I've been told numerous times. "Don't give me any of that Jesus talk ... that Jesus stuff isn't for me." Occasionally they'll highlight what that "Jesus stuff" was that turned them away. But it is never about the Jesus of the Gospels. It is what people have *done* with Jesus.

Seriously, in my entire life not a single person has registered a single complaint against the actual Jesus of the four Gospels. No one said to me, "You know, once he healed that leper and the hemorrhaging woman, I was done with him." Or "when he came out against lust, that was it for me. And that silly Lord's Prayer."

People like Jesus and admire him.

Jesus really isn't the problem, ever. But what people have done with Jesus turns many a stomach. Obviously churches, clergy by definition, and individual self-proclaimed Christians by extension, are considered spokespersons for Jesus. We can't say or do something without folks thinking that Jesus is behind it. Perhaps less so today than days gone by, but among church people this feeling is still strong. For example, at the heart of clergy sex abuse has been the hint, if not the outright declaration, that the person abusing their power is God's representative. That is not just in the Catholic Church. Clergy have power by virtue of their ordination, position, title. That gains clergy opportunity, influence, say-so. It allows David Koresh to sleep with anyone's wife or daughter in Waco, Jim Jones to get everyone to drink the Kool-Aid in Jonestown, and countless Father So-and-sos to abuse children without complaint or punishment.

Furthermore, too often Christian people offer insipid explanations for personal tragedies, making God, them and religion look awful. Jesus' people say and do a lot of non-Jesus stuff in Jesus' name, and not everyone catches the nuance, the contradiction, the hypocrisy. Instead, they feel the awful end result of hurtful religion or religious people, and attribute it to Jesus, and that's it for them. They're out the door, physically and spiritually. They won't be his sunbeam.

My Jesus

My very first funeral, a week after graduating from seminary, was for a stillborn baby born to unwed teenagers. Their very devout parents demanded an open casket funeral as a public shaming of their teenagers and to show what God had done to that baby in his divine disgust at their pre-marital shenanigans.

What happened to that couple? Did they go on to get married? Have kids? Were those kids baptized, raised in church, taught faith? Or when the teenagers got old enough, scarred beyond repair by a sadistic God and heartless parents, did they turn away from God's son and all his sunbeams?

My graffiti writer on some non-descript side street in Krakow had a front row seat for the excesses or outright failures of Jesus-based religion. The foundation for the Holocaust was carefully constructed by Christian Church teaching for centuries. Condemning Jews as "Christ-Killers" in hymn, scripture, liturgy and sacred pop culture, scapegoating Jews for any crisis to beset a town or village, isolating them from normal daily life – all this presaged the Holocaust. The painfully disturbing book, Daniel Goldhagen's *Hitler's Willing Executioners*, looks at how good, neighborly, everyday citizens became the willing executioners of their own Jewish friends and neighbors.

The graffiti writer was certainly not alive for the Holocaust or its lead-up. But we all live the aftermath. And frankly, when you walk the streets and breathe the air where evil has flourished, you feel it. You taste it. There's a reason old-time religion did exorcisms.

The graffiti, the writer, the song, and any of us can easily ask, where was the church? Where were the clergy? What came forth from the pulpit? In the centuries, years, days before the Holocaust and in the decades since, which Jesus was most front and center? Like all the Buddha images, we could come up with the Silent Jesus, the Three Monkey See-No-Evil, Hear-No-Evil, Speak-No-Evil Jesus, the Ostrich Head in the Sand Jesus, the Looking the Other Way Jesus, the Patriotic My Country Right or Wrong Jesus, and a Sunbeam Jesus.

You see why some folks, even graffiti artists and grunge rock stars, might turn away from that Jesus, or maybe Jesus all together?

Yes, there have been heroic exceptions. Individual priests sacrificed themselves for others. The Polish Pope John Paul II achieved sainthood in Poland long before the Church's stamp of approval. More ordinary Poles are acclaimed as "Righteous of the Gentiles" for saving Jews than from any other nationality. The Polish Solidarity pro-Democracy movement had vital clergy partners at great cost, including death.

Despite such exceptions, my guess is that for a lot of people there is a tipping point, and when they hit that point their faith tips over from real to "don't bother me with those stupid sunbeams."

For those of us still clinging to faith, we can't fully grasp why everyone else has wandered away. I look at my Jesus, and the world of faith I live in with that Jesus, and I can't imagine why everyone wouldn't want it.

My Jesus

I am a born evangelist. Whatever I am into, I extol to others. As Alida will tell you, any good experience I've just had is inevitably described as the best of all time. "That's the best movie I ever saw … this is the best Italian restaurant I've ever been at … that was the best vacation ever … I've never seen a more beautiful city!"

As a result, I simply cannot believe that someone wouldn't drop everything to go to my best restaurant, read my best ever novel, love my best ever rock band. How come you're not binge-watching the Netflix show I raved about? And embrace my Jesus? Trust me, he's the best God ever!

I look at my church. A quintessential, picture-perfect, New England congregational church as if imagined by Norman Rockwell. And who we are as a church is Norman Rockwell, too, an idealized vision of faith and community. We preach love so naturally it's like maple syrup running in the springtime. God is love. Love one another. Let's do a lot of good. You are forgiven. We affirm hard work, best practices, individual freedom. Jesus is our friend, kind and gentle, who calls us o'er the tumult. He died on the cross, but our altar cross is empty because we believe in happy endings.

We believe in Jesus, we believe in each other, we believe in Mom and apple pie, we make a big deal out of July 4 and Veteran's Day, we support our troops, we do good and help others, we do a good job with all the various Bible lists of things to do, we love children, bless animals, nurture terrific teens, and never forget the elderly.

So why would anyone skip church on a Sunday? Why go shopping, sleep in, play tennis, eat a bagel, read the paper? Anything but be with our Jesus? If ever a church was full of sunbeams, it is us.

But this Jesus of mine gets sidelined by Ugly Jesus. The most anti-Jesus Jesus people present themselves as the most fervently Jesus people, and their noise, their impact, their ugliness weighs more on any scale with a tipping point.

That Westboro Baptist Church in Kansas? Hardly anybody goes there. It's basically one hate-filled extended family. But their "God hates gays" campaign – using a word far cruder – carried more clout, gathered more attention, did more Jesus damage than anything my sweet church does to set the record straight. We went to a small museum in bucolic Ridgefield, Connecticut one lovely day for a quiet break. Inside was a photo display of Westboro Baptist Church anti-Jesus Jesus people spewing their Jesus-based hate at funerals of American soldiers killed in Iraq and Afghanistan. They declare that dead soldiers are God's punishment for a too gay-friendly USA. That ended our lovely day just as surely as they ruined the already heart-breaking funeral days of those soldiers' families. All in Jesus' name.

At one of the heights of anti-Muslim rhetoric in America a church group of so-called Christians from Texas showed up during Friday prayer outside a mosque near our town. Our Council of Churches asked local pastors to go and stand in solidarity with Muslims as they had to walk by protestors on the way to their prayers.

Observing and listening to their hostile words, I asked some Christian protestors what they were doing, and why? In particular, I had heard one person tell a young Muslim girl she was going to hell. That was precisely the purpose, the protester assured me, to save all those people from hell. When I suggested that there might be other ways more convincing than scaring the hell out of little kids and striking fear in the heart of Moms and Dads, our conversation ended.

I joined a few other pastors at the mosque entrance, saying "God bless you" to each worshipper coming or going. But who won the day as the face of Christ that day? As those Muslim children grow up or the adults age, whose Jesus is seared into their consciousness? The threat or blessing?

So much of the world's awfulness is perpetrated by people of faith in general, on behalf of some religion, in the name of some version of God. Too often that has been Jesus exploited, warped, twisted. Can you imagine the challenge of being an honorable Muslim right now, given the horrible excesses of evil done in Islam's name all over the world every day, one outrage after another? That's what it can be like presenting Jesus to people who ask about the role of Jesus in the Inquisition, slavery, the Crusades, the Holocaust, opposition to Civil Rights, opposition to gay people. Why are so many people, supposedly related to Jesus, so unloving?

The most contemporary example may be the rise of White Nationalism, Domestic Terrorism, gun-related mass killings. The link with Christianity, however tenuous or perverted, is still strong and visible. Our cross, our scriptures, our history are all fair game for those who yearn so enthusiastically to hate their neighbor. Prayer, Jesus' name, the Bible and Christian terminology are too often on prominent display during hateful events.

My Jesus gets outmaneuvered, outplayed, outflanked. Or more honestly, I do. By my ineffectiveness we leave Jesus to be portrayed by people who do more damage to Jesus than Pontius Pilate.

At least Pilate washed his hands of Jesus. But perverters of Jesus aim to embrace him, presenting him as their front man. And too many people cannot tell the difference.

Hatred, by itself, is evil. But I am focused on the hatred expressed in the name of Jesus' whole being.

I'd pay good money to see some pseudo-Christian with the courage of their convictions, not cloaked behind a fake faith, a false flag or a false Jesus. Could one of them stand up and say honestly, "I am Christian. My Christian faith is at least the seventh or eighth priority in my life. I definitely fit it in where it works well with my other six priorities: my race, my politics, my pocketbook, my nation, my party, my opinion." Instead, the abuse of immigrants, the neglect of the poor, the casual racism and anti-Semitism, the refusal to consider any steps toward gun safety, the apathy toward climate change, the opposition to social change are disturbingly cloaked in their idea of Jesus-faith.

There is also abuse of Jesus that is absurd or silly, that make people scratch their heads, or simply not take any

Jesus seriously who could be connected to such silliness. Jesus and God, in equal measure, get credited or blamed for losing a baseball game, scoring a touchdown, winning a football game, surviving a plane crash (without explaining what it means for those who didn't), an election that went your way (but never an election that went the other way). There are popstars wearing giant crosses while doing weird things. Watch religious TV for one day. Follow daily news stories as we do in our church, religiously, no pun intended. See theology and scripture twisted. See candidates line up their clergy. See the politician going into church, speaking at the pulpit, missing the altar call but leaving an offering, attending Mass, out before communion, on the way to the synagogue. Hear the "God Bless America" after every speech and "God Bless the First Responders" after every tragedy, followed by doing nothing.

From those same lips and that same thinking came absolute assurances that AIDS was God's punishment on homosexuals, and 9/11 was God's punishment for America's leniency toward feminists, the ACLU and liberalism.

At what point dare we call any hate-based religion what it is? When I've considered so-called Muslim or Islamic terrorism, I tried for years to call it what it is: anti-God, and child abuse. Deny terrorists the privilege of being known by faith, when their entire body of work is anti-faith, anti-God, anti-childhood. Strapping suicide vests on young women, forcing sexual slavery and early marriages, filling little kids with the abject filth of hate and love of murder, that is pure anti-God, anti-kid, anti-female, anti-sunbeam. Call it.

Likewise, among the abusers of Jesus. Their work is blasphemous, a heretical, false teaching, and a direct violation of the third commandment: "Thou shalt not take the name of the Lord thy God in vain." Exploiting Jesus, misquoting, misrepresenting Jesus, abusing Jesus as a political toy or a personal assistant, ascribing un-Jesus views to Jesus: all of this is wasting the holiness of God. Making it useless. Worthless. In vain. A sin. Call it.

No wonder my Krakow graffiti artist shouts with his paint can, "don't bother me with your sunbeam." Maybe Jesus doesn't want us for a sunbeam sometimes. Maybe sometimes Jesus wants us to be the point of the spear, or the thrust itself, or a two-fisted brawler. Or if not a sunbeam, then a thunderstorm; if not a happy stream of light, then a lightning strike. At least think about it.

Maybe we Jesus-people can be more like them, the Jesus-abuse Jesus people. More pointed, more abusive, better at P.R., louder, dramatic, grab the headlines, angry at everyone, wrapped in a flag, armed to the teeth, ready to rumble, mean-spirited, hard-edged. Maybe we need to take Jesus and his church back from those liberal God-is-Love-so-you-better-love-God / neighbor / stranger / alien / widow / orphan / leper / demon-possessed / hungry / thirsty / naked / imprisoned / paralytic / bleeding / seeking types.

Or maybe the graffiti writer and the Vaselines and Kurt Cobain need a hug. Maybe more sunbeams in Poland or Germany back in the dark days of yesteryear,

My Jesus

or now, would light up enough dark corners to brighten a whole room. Or church. Or town. Or nation. Or more.

St. John, in his gospel about Jesus, especially his uniquely poetic Christmas story (John 1:1-14) starts with an astounding declaration. "In the beginning was the Word...the word was God...in him was Life, and that life was the Light of the world. The Light shines in the Darkness and the Darkness has not overcome it" (John 1:1-5, NIV). Other versions have it, "the Darkness cannot comprehend it."

This really is my essential Jesus. Jesus, the Light, shines himself into the Darkness. And that Darkness, in all its manifestations, cannot comprehend it. Or overcome it. They are not of the same stuff, Darkness and Light. They do not mix well together. One will overwhelm the other. For Christ-followers that is Jesus, the Light.

In no way am I underestimating the power or presence of Darkness. Sickness, sorrow, despair, depression, injustice, poverty, mental health issues, economic struggles, family crisis, doubt, fear, loss – each of these can seem to blot out the sun, shut out the light, darken our day.

Years ago, a rage-filled man wearing yellow pants stood on a subway platform in New York City and pushed a promising Julliard School of Music flutist onto the subway tracks in front of an oncoming train. She survived but an arm was severed, ending her life's work and dream.

The next day the legendary journalist, Peter Hamill, wrote an article in the New York Daily News, with the headline, "The Devil Wore Yellow Pants."

Noted psychiatrist, Karl Menninger, after a lifetime devoted to mental illnesses, wrote a book, "Whatever Became of Sin?"

Both were pointing toward the reality and strength of Darkness. The Jesus at the heart of Christianity does not deny it, minimize it or rationalize it. Nor give in to it. He stands against it. The Darkness can neither comprehend the Light, which is Jesus, nor overcome it. Light wins.

There is the Darkness of death, and the Darkness of sin, and a whole host of forces who dare to mock a sunbeam as childish, weak, silly. Karl Marx likened faith to opium. Sigmund Freud equated it with a crutch. The Krakow graffiti writer dismisses a sunbeam faith, as if it were Santa Claus or the Tooth Fairy. Together, faith critics might argue that, while designed to give the immature temporary joys, in the long run they make us ill-prepared for the harsh realities of real life. That's one view.

Or we can embrace the sunbeam Light. We cannot only believe it, we can actively tout it, represent it, mirror it, reflect it, even turn it toward the darkness.

Sin and death are the two forces of Darkness. Sin is the stand-in word for every single one of life's regrets, every mess-up we make. The earliest late-night TV talk show host was Jack Paar. One member of his cast was a woman who read the baseball scores, usually summarized as Runs, Hits and Errors. But with her

My Jesus

enchanting European accent she would announce that the Yankees had seven Runs, nine Hits and two Mistakers. Mistakers is a softer word than sin, but both reflect an inability to do what we were supposed to do at any given moment. Most religious conversations reserve sin for obvious immorality, most especially of the sexual kind. So, we easily condemn the bank robber and rapist. But most people traverse life with mistakers not quite so glaring. The classic definition of sin is to miss the mark. Whenever the Bible sets a mark and we miss it by a mile or an inch, we still miss it. It is a sin, a mistaker, an error whether intentional or not. When Jesus tells us to go the extra mile and we go the extra foot, or to feed the hungry and we don't have time, or to be humble and our arrogance gets in the way, or any of a hundred other marks set for our attainment and we fall short, or fail to try, or ignore entirely – that's sin. As life goes on, the mistakes and regrets pile up. This can result in guilt, stress, despair, shame, fear. The more genuine you are, the more aware of sin's Darkness you are. Jesus' life, death and resurrection are meant precisely to send a sunbeam directly into the face of that Darkness and overcome it.

Sin's theological twin is death, the ultimate Darkness. The Bible has two drop-dead statements that go hand in hand, leaving us in a bad position. "All have sinned and fall short of the glory of God" (Romans 3:23) puts us all uncomfortably in the same boat. Wait, it gets worse. "And the wages of sin is death" (6:23). In other words, we all miss the mark, and the penalty is that we are out of the game. Over is over.

It is starting to sound like Kurt Cobain was right when he sang "'cause sunbeams aren't made like me." Such negativity and doom go together well.

Unless.

Unless the Sunday School kids' version is our true reality. Perhaps it is so, that

> Jesus wants us for a sunbeam
> To shine each day
> In every way
> At home, at school, at play.
> I can if I but try
> Then live with Him on High.

The darkness of Death is oh so real in those moments of greatest loss. I've been there, repeatedly. And I never underestimate the enemy, another Biblical name for death.

But never underestimate the power of Light, in all its manifestations.

I will end with the near end of the Bible, Revelation 21. The Bible begins with creation. "In the beginning God created," (Genesis 1:1), getting the universe off on a good start. "It is good," God declared. Then follow thousands of years of Biblical history, humanity's ups and downs, millennia of mistakes by nations and religions and merchants and citizens. You name it, it's in the Bible. Horrors, famines, slaughters, injustices and indignity to the nth degree.

My Jesus

By the time of Revelation 21 God has intervened in human history, showed disgust, meted out punishment, and renewed the universe to its original joy.

It is Paradise, again.

Revelation's description of Paradise is purposefully over the top: streets paved with gold, no more tears, twelve gates to the city each made of a single pearl.

Somewhat overlooked is the presence of unparalleled light. "It (Heaven, Paradise) shone with the glory of God, its brilliance was like that of a very precious jewel...it does not need the sun or the moon to shine on it, for the glory of God gives it light, and the Lamb (Jesus) is its lamp. The nations will walk by its light...for there will be no night there" (Revelation 21:11, 23-25).

Until then, Jesus does want you for a sunbeam.

SEVEN

Lists of Kerygma

One afternoon three strangers rang my doorbell, looking for a Bible Study. Each had a story and a need.

One was fresh off a miracle. An opera singer, he had been on tour when he took sick. Stuck in a hotel room, his tour threatened, his career at risk, he opened the end table next to his bed. What he found changed his life forever. A Gideon Bible.

The Gideons are famous for one thing: giving away Bibles. Without being judgmental, without pressure, without gimmicks they merely and literally "spread the word". Outside schools, in remote areas around the world, in hotel end tables, people are offered a Bible.

My friend, the opera singer, opened the Bible, found some verses about healing, put himself in God's hands, and was healed. He could sing. When the tour ended, he determined to find a Bible Study, which led him to my front door. His decision to trust God, to follow up with a commitment to study, and to jump into our church life fully was undoubtedly the key factor in reviving that New York City church.

His two friends were more interested in a formula. They were familiar with Buddhism, and Buddha's helpful lists. There are The Three Universal Truths (nothing is ever lost, everything changes, Karma – cause and effect).

My Jesus

Add The Four Noble Truths (there is suffering, there is desire or attachment, we can eliminate attachment, and the path to do it is Eightfold). And the Noble Eightfold Path is right view, right resolve, right speech, right conduct, right livelihood, right effort, right mindfulness, right union or meditation. These lists are practical, useful guides for daily life.

The two friends, inspired by the opera singer's conversion, were hoping for a Christian parallel to Buddha's lists. Meaning no disrespect at all, they wanted a "Six Easy Steps to Being a Christian."

We have that. Christianity may not brand it as such, but we have St. Paul's nine "Fruits of the Spirit" (love, joy, peace, patience, kindness, goodness, faithfulness, gentleness, self-control, Galatians 5:22-23). We have Jesus' Beatitudes, his own eightfold path to true happiness (Blessed are the poor in spirit, they that mourn, the meek, those who hunger and thirst for righteousness, the merciful, the pure in heart, the peacemakers and the persecuted, Matthew 5:3-10). God's Ten Commandments are clearly designed to chart out the right life in connection with society, family and God (Exodus 20).

But when Jesus was asked pointblank, "Teacher, what must I do to gain eternal life?", his answer becomes known as the Two Great Commandments: "Love God in every way possible, and love your neighbor as you love yourself" (Luke 10:25-37).

We have the Ten Commandments, Nine Fruits of the Spirit, Eight Beatitudes, Two Great Commandments. Can we go one number lower? After affirming those Two Great Commandments Jesus says, in effect, that says it all. "On this hang all the law and the prophets". Yet Jesus does himself one better, offering The Golden Rule. In Luke's version of the Sermon on the Mount, Jesus states a radical path of ethical behavior.

> Love your enemies,
> do good to those who hate you,
> bless those who curse you,
> pray for those who mistreat you ...
> turn your other cheek ...
> give to everyone who asks.

Then the clincher is the one-rule bottom line, "do unto others as you would have them do unto you" (Luke 6:27-31).

Buddha and Jesus were walking a similar path. While Buddha may have been less focused on God than Jesus was, they both were saying that the best way to be right with the universe or its Creator is to be right with everything around you. And the key to that is to be less hung up on yourself and more in tune with the world around you, and the Creator.

There is nothing wrong with wanting lists or having them. Mnemonic devices help us to remember what is essential. What is essential can be presented in ways that make it simple and clear, though not easy. Done well, you end up with a faith that is well-designed, interconnected, and makes sense.

At our church we emphasize St. John's seminal teaching, "God is love" (1 John 4:8,16) and the word

My Jesus

borrowed from my Indian colleague, Azariah, "Christlikeness". Both are true and brief and largely self-explanatory. Yet, if those are the bones of our faith it does help to put some meat on them. These various lists do that. If God is love, and the best way for us to emulate God's love is to live a Christlike life, then it helps to have specifics to go with it – the what and the how.

Jesus' Nazareth sermon, his "Final Exam", and the Great Commission handle the what. At Nazareth, in his hometown synagogue, he read the prophet Isaiah's dramatic job description of the Messiah:

> The Spirit of the Lord is on me because he has anointed me to preach good news to the poor, to proclaim freedom for the prisoners, and recovery of sight to the blind; to release the oppressed, and to proclaim the year of the Lord's favor.
>
> (Luke 4:18-19)

Then he shocked everyone by saying, in effect, that's me doing my job (verse 21).

That was at the beginning of his public career. Three years later, nearing the end of his human life, he offers an equally dramatic job description, transferring responsibility from him to us. Jesus likens humanity to sheep and goats, each headed to their just reward based on simple and direct acts of compassion. Those who feed the hungry, give water to the thirsty, clothe the naked, and visit the sick and lonely and imprisoned are welcomed into the Kingdom expressly created for them (Matthew 25:31-46). And those who neglect the obvious

Lists of Kerygma

opportunities to be Christlike "go away", Jesus says, "to eternal punishment." This "Final Exam" is pass/fail.

Taking Jesus' two-sided job description, his and ours, literally and figuratively, we have plenty of specifics to keep us busy.

With his job on earth completed, and the hand-off to us completed, Jesus arrives at his Ascension Day. But before his feet leave the earth, he has a final say, known as the Great Commission:

> All authority in heaven and on earth has been given to me. Therefore go and make disciples of all nations, baptizing them in the name of the Father and of the Son and of the Holy Spirit, and teaching them to obey everything I have commanded you. And surely I am with you always. (Matthew 28:18-20)

That's a wrap. He's done doing it for us. We are now a team. Jesus will work through us, he will push and cajole, he will remind and empower. But the onus is on us to walk in his footsteps, emulating his life in word and deed. At the Lord's Last Supper he had said, "I've set you an example that you should do as I have done" (John 13:15). Even more startling, Jesus adds, "whoever believes in me will do the works I have been doing, and <u>they will do even greater things</u> than these" (John 14:12).

Returning to the Buddha-like lists, Jesus and the Bible lay out reasonable expectations for our daily life once we choose to be Christlike to the best of our ability.

My Jesus

This is captured perfectly in a succession of verses from St. John's Epistles. The New York Times has an author interview feature that ends with, "In fifty words convince the reader to read your book." These verses are like that, providing the convincing heart of this book.

> How great is the love the Father has lavished on us, that we should be called children of God (1 John 3:1). This is the message you heard from the beginning. We should love one another.
>
> (1 John 3:11)

> This is how we know what love is: Jesus laid down his life for us. And we ought to lay down our lives for one another. If anyone has material possessions and sees his brother (or sister) in need, but has no pity on him, how can the love of God be in him? Dear children, let us not love with words or tongue, but with actions and in truth.
>
> (1 John 3:16-18)

> Dear friends, let us love one another, for love comes from God. Everyone who loves has been born of God and knows God. Whoever does not love does not know God because God is love. This is how God showed his love among us: God sent his one and only Son into the world that we might live through him. This is love; not that we loved God, but that God loved us and sent his Son as an atoning sacrifice for our sins. Dear friends since God so loved us, we also ought to love one another. No one has ever seen God, but if we love one

Lists of Kerygma

> another, God lives in us and his love is made complete in us. (1 John 4:7-12)
>
> God is love. Whoever lives in love lives in God and God in them. In this way, love is made complete among us ... because in this world we are like him. There is no fear in love. But perfect love drives out fear. (1 John 4:16b-18a)
>
> We love because God first loved us. (1 John 4:19)
>
> This is how we know that we love the children of God: by loving God and carrying out God's commands. This is love for God: to obey God's commands are not burdensome. (1 John 5:2-3)

I first put those verses together when writing my biography of Azariah. Looking to summarize his breathtaking ministry among the poor in India, I asked him for his favorite Bible verse. He made it easy, responding, "Oh, all the verses about love". That led me to this section of scripture that offers a perfect circle. God loves us. God takes the initiative. The proof of that love is the gift of Jesus. Our best response to God, our best "thank you", is to love others. By so doing we enter into the absolute essence of God, for "God is love". It's not just that God likes love or prefers love or endorses love or wants love. God is love. That is definitional, foundational, essential. This wonderful, scriptural circle is completed when "we love because God first loved us" (1 John 4:19).

The direct result of this wisdom circle from St. John is that we know that whatever is loving is Godly. Whatever isn't, isn't. Try applying that to daily life and see how it helps sort things out fairly clearly.

My Jesus

In addition, there are seven "I Ams" in which Jesus gives definitive statements of who he is.

All from the Gospel of John, all begin with "I Am", they are, in order:

- ✓ I Am the Bread of Life, John 6:36
- ✓ I Am the light of the world, John 8:12
- ✓ I Am the Door (Gate), John 10:9
- ✓ I Am the Good Shepherd, John 10:11
- ✓ I Am the Resurrection and the Life, John 11:25-26
- ✓ I Am the way, the truth, and the life, John 14:6
- ✓ I Am the vine, you are the branches, John 15:5

It could be that Jesus is using a popular preacher's device, repetition: "I am, I am, I am". Or it could be that this Trinitarian-aware Son remembered that the Trinitarian-aware Father had made a quite similar response to Moses. Moses had been given the frightening job of confronting Egypt's Pharaoh to demand the freedom of all the Jews. When Moses wanted to know "who shall I say sent me?", God said, "I Am that I Am. Tell Pharaoh 'I Am sent me'" (Exodus 3:14).

To declare "I Am" is also the best way to define oneself, instead of letting everyone else have a go at it. Jesus may well be The Cosmic Christ, the Mirror of the Eternal and the Ground of All Being. But he says that he is the Light that lets you see, the gate that keeps you safe, the Good Shepherd who looks after you, the Bread of Life that nourishes you, the Resurrection that enlivens you now and forever, the Way and Truth and Life that guide you, the Vine that connects you. In seven neat sentences he describes what we need, what is vital and urgent, what is better than the alternative, what will help us. He takes us from the mundane to the eternal, from the personal to the universal. And he tells us that he is in the middle of it all.

As seen earlier, Christians and theologians have long argued about the "nature" of Jesus (God, man, or both); and if divine, when did he know it?

These "I Ams," crescendoing with "Resurrection, Way, Truth, and Life", show him with a clear sense of purpose, identity, destiny. He offers a path to the best experience of life in this life in ways that we are fulfilled, and in the promise of life after this life when our greatest enemy, fear itself, fear of death, is taken away. Jesus is not soft peddling himself.

What's more, he links his destiny and ours together. Together, we are the proof of each other. A shepherd without sheep, sheep without a shepherd are both left wandering. Vine and branches cut off from each other end the reason for each. But together, we are symbiotic. We are one.

In short order, he opens the door, brightens our path, watches over us along the way, sustains and nourishes us lest we grow weak or weary, revives us when necessary, guides us faithfully, and never lets go. That is the "way" Jesus offers.

From the world of classic rock, The Who asked, "Who are You?" Peter Frampton offers a love song response with a theological parallel:

>I'm in you.

You're in me.
You gave the love, the love that I never had.

Pop culture once again reveals more than it may have known. The ultimate I Am of Jesus is that simple: "I'm in you. You're in me."

Biblically, we see that most clearly in his miracles. Jesus is a presence and a power that move seamlessly from the incarnated Jesus to the person in need being incarnated by Jesus.

Consider two archetypical healings. The first is Jesus' encounter with a woman weakened by eighteen years of bleeding, leaving her perpetually unclean by the custom of the day, and therefore isolated, ostracized. She approaches Jesus within a large crowd, stoops low, unseen, to merely touch the hem of his garment. Jesus responds with an intriguing question and an even more intriguing statement. "Who touched me?" he asked. He said he felt "virtue" go out of him (Mark 5:30, King James Version). Virtue, some essential part of his nature, a surge of energy, transferred out of Jesus into a person yearning to be whole. What was with him was now with her. The I am of Jesus became the I am of the woman in need.

When I asked Alida what Bible story most captures the essential Jesus for her, she said "the bent over woman." Read it and know.

> On a Sabbath Jesus was teaching in one of the synagogues, and a woman was there who had been crippled by a spirit for eighteen years. She was bent over and could not straighten up at all. When Jesus

saw her, he called her forward and said to her, "Woman, you are set free from your infirmity." Then he put his hands on her, and immediately she straightened up and praised God. Indignant because Jesus had healed on the Sabbath, the synagogue leader said to the people, "There are six days for work. So come and be healed on those days, not on the Sabbath." The Lord answered him, "You hypocrites! Doesn't each of you on the Sabbath untie your ox or donkey from the stall and lead it out to give it water? Then should not this woman, a daughter of Abraham, whom Satan has kept bound for eighteen long years, be set free on the Sabbath day from what bound her?" When he said this, all his opponents were humiliated, but the people were delighted with all the wonderful things he was doing. (Luke 13:10-17)

Each healing and miracle story by Jesus has a "wow!" factor, but often their real force is in presaging something far greater. Jesus is never "just" calming a storm, feeding a multitude, driving out demons, or healing a woman with a long history of bleeding. Each says, look deeper, think bigger.

Think through the elements of this story. Sabbath. Crippled woman. Jesus. Healing. Criticism. Wonder.

With the "Blue Laws" long gone from America, which kept Sunday special for generations, people cannot grasp how holy, sacred, set apart the Sabbath used to be, and is meant to be. By definition, by God's command, it is meant to be different from every other day in every way.

My Jesus

In that light, look at what Jesus does. First, he notices a woman "bent over, crippled by a spirit for eighteen years." My guess is that, when first stricken, people in town felt bad for her. Sympathy may have lasted for weeks. After a while, people's attention moved on to other needs, other people. After eighteen years she was part of the scenery. In another miracle in Mark 8 a blind man, partially healed, tells Jesus that he "sees people, but they look like trees walking." That was life for this woman in her village, a bent-over tree walking. A person, yes. But really just part of the scenery. No one took notice.

Jesus noticed.

Jesus called her forward. Throughout his life he called people forward. Out of crowds, out of hiding, out of shame, out of work, out of routine, out of prejudice, out of ego. He finds you where you are and calls you forward.

What was her problem? This is a preacher's paradise. Her bent back and inability to stand up tall can be a fill-in for every form of burden. Crushed under the weight of ... burdened by ... weighed upon ... debt, worries, baggage, sin.

John Bunyan's *Pilgrim's Progress* describes the pilgrim, Christian by name, as increasingly bent over as he travels through life, each failure adding to the burden he bears. Until. Arriving at the foot of the cross, barely able to look up, Christian sees Jesus and Christian's knapsack of burdens falls away. At last he stands up, a new man, with a new perspective.

Luke says the bent-over woman was crippled by a spirit. With no known obvious cause, like falling off a

Lists of Kerygma

donkey, ancient times assumed evil spirits at work, or bad karma. You got what you deserve, either because you deserve it, or your parents deserve you to deserve it. Jesus rejects that thinking elsewhere, but here ignores it. What matters is his Kerygma. He will have a story happen, then draw out a lesson that should keep people thinking, and doing, until he returns. Until then, we must ask how this miracle speaks to us in our day amidst our issues.

Think of people bent over for such a long time, no way to stand up tall, they can't face the day head on, the weight of whatever is too heavy, and now they are hardly noticed. Is that a thing in our world?

It doesn't take long before we are in hard political territory. Student debt. Medical costs. Refugees. Immigrants. Racism. Poor schools. Opioid crisis. Addictions, plural. Aging population. Terrorism, domestic and foreign. Endless war. All these issues and a dozen more cripple us.

And here's Jesus saying, "Come here. I need you to stand up tall." He says that to a woman, to a hopeless case, on the Sabbath, interrupting worship, creating a scene, breaking the law, drawing condemnation from the authorities. Just another day at the office for my Jesus.

The lists of Jesus' stories and miracles and sayings are his lived kerygma. They show the way.

"Jesus is the way" was a popular bumper sticker. Yes, indeed. But how that way is followed, where that way leads is not as simplistic as the bumper sticker implied in its heyday. In that same "Jesus movement" era, it was

My Jesus

popular to raise the pointer finger in the air when worshipping or referring to Jesus, letting it be known that Jesus is not only the way but THE way, the only way. The affirmation was a denial that any other spiritual guide or religious leader or religion by itself had anything to offer.

Practitioners of this denial went ever further, then and now. The "only way" Jesus of their finger-pointing and bumper stickers comes with a set of stringent rules and doctrines, and you are either all in or all out.

While still a Baptist I took my youth group mountain climbing. After, they wanted to play frisbee. Happily, I found a Baptist summer camp closed for the autumn. At the Director's office I asked if we Baptists could use his empty Baptist fields to play frisbee. He was delighted and welcoming. Reaching into his desk he produced a statement of doctrine with twenty-five items, all of which I had to affirm with a signature. All twenty-five. Or no frisbee.

They had found their way. Interestingly, it included none of Jesus' seven "I Ams", none of his eight Beatitudes or two Great Commandments or one Golden Rule or Paul's nine Fruits of the Spirit. As I said, they had found their way. Not much of Jesus'.

Jesus' way is his Kerygma, his proclamation of what is important and how to achieve it. He lived it, he did it. And there weren't twenty-five doctrinal statements in order to enter "the Kingdom prepared for you since the creation of the world" (Matthew 25:34). Christlikeness is Jesus' Kerygma, and ours.

EIGHT

God as Opera

Why am I so focused on Jesus? It is almost to the exclusion of the Holy Spirit, accompanied by a respectful distance from God. Yet I am a monotheist; I accept and believe in the oneness of God while still a Trinitarian even if I cannot adequately explain it. The closest I ever came to explaining the Trinity was using a large-size children's picture book about an apple. Page 1 showed a single juicy red apple. Over the next few pages that one apple gets peeled, sliced, cored. On the last page you have a pile of peelings, several slices, scattered seeds, and the core. How many apples are there on the table, we are asked? Still one, naturally. That's the Trinity. Begins as one, ends as one, but in the middle gets broken up into the saving, redemptive, physical, earthly life of Jesus; and the ongoing, inspiring, comforting, guiding work of the Holy Spirit. All set in motion by Creator God. Apple, flesh and seeds. Got it? Close enough.

I'm the flesh guy. God in the flesh. God in the nitty-gritty. God in Jesus.

On a trip to Paris, we toured the magnificent Opera House. I'm not an opera fan, I say ignorantly, never having been to one. With ignorance comes prejudice, so I've avoided opera. The tour was great fun. You saw the splendor and spectacle and could easily imagine the grandness of *Aida* leaving everyone breathless.

My Jesus

Even better was the next day. At the Musée d'Orsay our guide took us to a cutaway scale model of the Opera House. You still imagine Chagall's awesome ceiling, the ornate hall, the glitzy private boxes, the sense of grandeur, even if it was cut open and split down the middle. The fun was just beginning. The sliced-in-half miniature Opera House continued from up above the stage, and behind the curtains, to down below, into the bowels and basement, and even, Phantom-lovers, the pond. Pulleys and weights, ropes, staging, lifts, scenery, tunnels. Suddenly, all the grandeur of opera on the stage makes sense because of all that happens down below making sense.

Jesus makes sense.

In Jesus, with Jesus, through Jesus the machinations of God come to light in a way that reintroduces us to God.

The very humanity of Jesus forces us into the details. It's popular to say, "the Devil is in the details," but I prefer "Jesus is in the details."

With an Omniscient, Omnipotent, Omnipresent yet remote God it is possible to read in the Biblical story of Noah that God was fed up with humankind and decided to kill everyone and everything except Noah's family and a reproductive two-some of each species. Knowing Jesus makes us shout "Time out" midway through the Genesis 6:9-7:23 story and ask some detailed questions.

Put Jesus in the Sodom and Gomorrah story just before two towns are thoroughly wiped out, and Lot's wife is turned into salt (Genesis 19). Put Jesus in Egypt just before the Angel of Death kills every first-born

Egyptian child (Exodus 11-12). Put Jesus in the story of slaughtering 500 pagan priests after they lost a bet with Elijah (1 Kings 18:40).

Lots of Bible stories and our personal stories cry out for the presence of the Jesus we know from the Gospels. Maybe as a correction, maybe as a "yes, but ...", maybe as a protest, maybe as a minority opinion that was overruled.

A child dies. Some Christian friend or pastor tells the parents "God needed a beautiful flower for his garden ... another angel in heaven." It may be that in the year 840, 1260 or 1531 a totally devastated mom and dad found solace in the thought that their child was frolicking in God's garden. Sort of an ancient version of valium.

But when we look straight at Jesus, we know full well that God doesn't look down on earth scouring for children to yank out of their parent's arms because God is so lonely for new angels, and the Creator of the Universe is incapable of growing his own garden without stealing from yours.

In other words, there are lots of images of God that don't stand up to the close inspection offered by knowing Jesus. Harsh, arbitrary, vindictive, violent, hateful, unreasonable acts are attributed to God without question for thousands of years across many scriptures in just about every religion. And lots of us take it without question because it is sacred.

But just as every religion has literalists and fundamentalists who seemingly worship every noun, verb and adjective in their Holy Writ, there have always

My Jesus

been prophets and scholars and renegade believers who emulated Jacob. Jacob wrestled with God, literally, battling to a draw (Genesis 32:22-32). That can be our invitation to wrestle with God-stories, enlightened by time, context, study, inspiration, wisdom – and Jesus.

Perhaps people are afraid that if we don't accept certain verses hook, line and sinker, even if they make us squirm, what will happen to our favorite verses that make someone else squirm?

We've created a holy equivalence Catch-22. If we believe that Jesus healed the blind man then we are required to believe that God told the Israelites to slaughter every man, woman, child, elderly person and animal in Jericho (Joshua 6:21). Or if we believe that Jesus said, "blessed are the pure in heart," then we must also accept that God ordered the town elders to stone to death a disobedient child (Deuteronomy 21: 18-21). And for the Virgin Birth and the Resurrection to have happened then must we also believe that God induced famine, plague and war to teach people a lesson?

Such equivalency is not a necessity for faith or salvation.

Jesus does not think, act or talk that way. If, in Christian teaching, we believe that Jesus is the Son of God, very God, part of the Godhead, pre-existent with God the Father and the Holy Spirit, an equal part of the three-in-one, then we need to know this Jesus. To know Jesus is to be willing to wrestle with words, stories, scriptures that predate him or exclude him; to use the

God as Opera

Jesus we know as our guide to all of faith's writ and history.

In another age I might have been burned at the stake along with my Czech hero, Jan Hus, for heresy, for ideas not up someone else's alley. I have at least two such ideas.

Before being ordained I first had to present a lengthy Ordination Paper, one that laid out my beliefs. All the standard Protestant Baptist stuff, which I was at the time. To the committee's dismay, I suggested that God's interaction with humanity had changed over time. Parents change as they have more children, and as the children grow up. We don't parent the first child the way we do the third. Our day-to-day relationships with our 15-year-old boy child is not the same as with our 6-year-old girl child. We adjust, trying to get through, trying to relate, trying to be understood, trying to connect. God, too, I suggested. Didn't Jesus tell us to call God "Our Father," even Abba, Dad?

Now, I'm not entirely stupid. It may well be, probably is, that it is us, we fallible, gullible humans, who have matured over time in our understanding of God. Maybe God was always the gracious Jesus of the Gospels, and it took us a few millennia to catch on. But I was twenty-four at the time, working from the Bible as my foundation. My argument was something akin to, okay, God starts out strong, stern, do it right the first time or else. After kicking Adam and Eve out of Eden, wiping the earth clean with Noah's Flood, God starts over. Next, he tries the "Great Man Theory of History," that history is the story of great men striding across the stage of civilization. So,

My Jesus

we get Abraham, Isaac, Jacob, Joseph, Moses. People still aren't getting it. Humans need more specific boundaries and crystal-clear explanations. Thus, the Ten Commandments, followed by a few thousand more laws in exquisite detail. And Judges to spell it all out. Then Kings and nationhood and organized religion to enforce and encourage it.

Not good enough. People are still constantly looking for loopholes, living the letter of the law, not the spirit, and then sacrificing animals to make up for every sin. Tough on the animals and does not really change anybody. Nobody ever was dissuaded from coveting his neighbor's maidservant because then he'd have to sacrifice an ox. So, the Prophets. God sends bold spokesmen who unabashedly explain the spirit behind God's laws. With a carrot and stick approach, the Isaiahs and Jeremiahs of the Bible, and Amos and Micah, take people to the heart of religion. "You know, O human, what is good, and what the Lord requires. Do justice, love mercy, walk humbly … let justice roll down like waters, and righteousness like an ever-flowing stream" (Micah 6:8; Amos 5:24).

Close, but no cigar.

Exasperated, God says, in effect, let me go down there myself and show them how it's done. That is how we get Jesus. Remember, Jesus is the fulfillment of the Isaiah 7:14 prophecy, that the Messiah would be "Emmanuel, which means 'God with us'." If Jesus is "God with us" then it certainly appears that God's approach to us changes, just as our approaches change as parents.

Sternness, punishment, rules, lectures have their place and their time. But with Jesus it all changes from "Because I said so" to "let's do this together."

That poor Ordination Committee was in a tizzy. I was grilled relentlessly until an old West Virginia Baptist interrupted and declared "I think we've tortured this boy long enough. I vote to ordain him." Whether the idea of God's development is heresy or not, I don't know how else to take us from a God of mass slaughter, extreme vindictiveness and arbitrary prejudice to Jesus on the cross because "God so loved the world" that he forgave those "who know not what they do" (John 3:16 Luke 23:34).

That Jesus is my answer to every questioner, doubter, skeptic, agnostic, cynic, atheist, ex-believer, angry, recovering Christian I have ever met. I don't claim any great record in converting the masses of non-believers. But the Jesus of our ministry has enabled people to give their all to faith and church and mission with an amazing depth.

This Jesus is my second heresy, which came about through running. I was an avid runner, daily for forty plus years, until the knees gave out. That was before iPhones, ear buds and podcasts. Running could get boring, as much as I loved it and the runner's high that came with it.

On a spiritual retreat a Catholic nun suggested I come up with a mantra, a faith-based phrase I could mutter while running. To my very Protestant amazement, it worked. That afternoon I went on a long run, came up with a short prayer-like phrase, started repeating it, and finished that day's run faster and more refreshed. This established a pattern of praying while running.

Over time I noticed that I would talk with God in general terms about general things. But when it came to specifics, I found myself concentrating on Jesus. It was not intentional at first, though now it is; then it seemed natural. God has a job to do, Jesus has a job to do, the Holy Spirit has a job to do. Let them do their jobs. They may all be One Triune God, but we have different words for each, different Bible stories and verses, different adjectives and nouns for each.

Which is why, on one of those long runs, I used my running prayer time to ask God for two favors. Note, I went to God for permission. To some degree I was renegotiating my contract with God as a pastor, as God's servant. I had just re-entered pastoral life after a corporate role at Habitat for Humanity, and some changes were in order. The twists and turns of Christian life led me to seek permission. First, I wanted God to allow and bless a pastoral ministry that would, from that day on, err on the side of loving too much rather than too little. I had spent too much time with Christians whose love was too limited. They seemed to have little to do with the Jesus of the Cross whose forgiveness was alarmingly universal. Second, I asked God to let me focus the rest of my pastoral career on Jesus. That has ramifications. Above all, it means that Jesus is the prism through which I read and use the whole rest of the Bible. The writings of Paul, the Book of Leviticus, the ramblings of Ecclesiastes, the visions of Revelation all take on a different shade when held up to the light of Jesus. After all, if Jesus is "the light of the world" (John 8:12), put that light to work.

Yes, the arrogance is stunning, that occurred to me years later. I was asking the Creator of the Universe, the First Person of the Trinity, to allow me to prioritize the Second Person over the First and the Third.

Nevertheless, I did. This prayer negotiation went on over the course of several days and, in true prayer fashion, allowed for plenty of give and take. God made me work for it. Mile by mile I laid out my rationale for prioritizing love and Jesus.

To be blunt, I told God it was all I could grasp. After a lifetime and career fully immersed in the broadest spectrum of Christianities (yes, plural), plus personal experience and study of world religions, and having been taught by great preachers and teachers, I had not found anything more compelling than the love of God as experienced through the life and teachings of Jesus.

Jesus is my best expression of God. I was asking permission not to leave his side. It is that idea of being so connected that leads to the popular phrase, "What Would Jesus Do?" That, and its acronym WWJD, are so overused they have lost their clout. They shouldn't.

Do you know their origin story? In the late 1800's Charles Sheldon was a congregationalist pastor in Topeka, Kansas. Moved by the plight of the poor and his Biblical commitment to the social gospel (applying the gospel to society), Sheldon preached a series of sermons that were serialized in a Chicago newspaper. Collected as *In His Steps: What Would Jesus Do*, it told the story of a

My Jesus

pastor deeply moved by the death of a homeless man who had been in his church the previous Sunday. The pastor challenged his congregation to live the next year entirely guided by one question: What would Jesus do? The novel tells the story of church members who take up the challenge.

What I've done, theologically and biblically, is to take that to the nth degree. No one would suggest I am close to that ideal, but it is still the ideal.

If Jesus fleshes out God two thousand years ago, we flesh out Jesus today.

If Jesus is God, then we are invited, not forced but invited, to see God in a new way. If Jesus isn't God, well, so much for this book, the Trinity, Christianity, a lot of great music, and several trillion prayers. It is Jesus who makes it possible for us to know the inner workings of God.

Which brings us back to the Trinity. How do we keep it all together, three-in-one, with our monotheism intact? My guess is with scotch tape, the clear kind. We can stick the Three Persons of the Trinity side by side and each will be clear yet linked.

Trinitarian Christianity is lofty theological thinking, and not easy. There are stupefying yet inspiring medieval religious paintings with God way up above, way, way up there; Jesus down here, close to us, close to earth; the Holy Spirit, dove-like, soars about, up and down as need be. The Trinity in action, three distinct actors and actions, one God.

God as Opera

For me it is much like the Virgin Birth and the episode of Jesus walking on the water (Matthew 14:25-31). I believe it all, and it is not uncritical belief or blind faith. I've worked through them, and still do. They are matters of faith, each a stretch. That's what faith is, usually, a stretch from the norm, from what is obvious or explicable. None of the three (Trinity, Virgin Birth, walking on water) are essential to salvation. Therefore, they can be set aside, if one wishes or needs. I don't wish or need. They are part of the mystery of God, and the mystery of faith, and there is enough rationale for each that I choose to enter the mystery.

Jesus walked on water one day, somehow, for a purpose important enough to set aside the normal relationship between a person and a large body of water. What should be sinking or swimming became, with Jesus, walking. With the Virgin Birth, God entered the human condition through the very physical life of Mary. "The Holy Spirit will come upon you," was the angel's explanation, without explaining anything. There will be no human, male sexual contact as we know it. Yet there will be a union, an intimacy, and a very recognizable end result baby as we know it. Jesus is the result however you imagine the birth.

Jesus gives rise to Christianity which has conceptualized God in ways that allow us to see God's variety and unity. We have God as Creator, Jesus the Savior, Holy Spirit the energizer. God chooses to function with multiple aspects, and we experience these aspects in ways that speak to us, sometimes literally, or connect with us

My Jesus

figuratively. Somehow it works, by faith. We don't need faith to explain the obvious.

Which brings us to anthropomorphism, the idea that God is best explained/understood in human terms. Certainly, in my seminary days, to be anthropomorphistic was proof of a simple mind, a very "lite" theologian, a primitive and undeveloped faith. Anthropomorphism is expressed in stock phrases like "put yourself in God's hands" or hymns like "His Eye is on the Sparrow", as if God has hands and eyes like us. Special disdain was reserved for hymns or ideas that imagined a personal, unique relationship between you and God. One dear professor lectured for an entire hour against the hymn "In the Garden," which declares

> I come to the garden alone...
> And he walks with me
> And talks with me
> And tells me I am his own.
> ("In the Garden," C. Austin Miles, 1912)

This was at a time when modern Christians were reacting to "God is Dead" Sixties theology with new talk of God as the Ground of All Being, the Universal Truth, Universal Life Force, The Prime Mover, the Infinite. So, there was no room for thinking you could sit in a park and get a divine hug from one part of the Trinity or another. Get over it, was the idea, get over yourself. God is not your personal friend, savior, banker, Santa Claus, gofer, or personal anything. God is greater. Nowadays that phrase "greater" has been embraced and popularized to read "God is greater than your need," a good thing. Your situation, your crisis, your addiction, your problem, your sorrow pales in comparison to God's wondrous ability to enter your predicament, to sidle up next to you, take your hand, guide you along, pick you up if necessary. God is that much greater.

My seminary professor allowed no such sunny side. The point then was that God is greater than you can imagine, so stop imagining, stop trying to sidle up, stop waiting for that hug. God is above your need. Not really as comforting, nor meant to be.

There's some good Biblical theology behind dehumanizing God. In the scriptures God's name is initially unutterable. YHWH. Then, with the Ten Commandments, God's name is not to be used idly, "in vain", and God is not to be imaged in any way, which is just a few letters away from not being imagined.

I get that. But I don't accept that. You want to burn me at the stake? Let me give you some firewood. I am moving further and further away from God as spirit and force and energy and closer to Joan Osborne's 1995 song, "What if God Was One of Us?"

Don't light the firewood, yet. I did not say that God is not spirit, force, energy. In the Genesis creation story, God's spirit hovers over the face of the earth before God's creative energy bursts forth with such force that the Big Bang Theory can't begin to describe it. Huge forests, tall mountains, deep oceans, vast resources, infinite varieties of infinite life. Every minute of creation was a Northern Lights explosion and a Grand Canyon "wow."

The God of all that has every right to assume that would be enough. Create the world, set it in order, place us in charge, go on to other universes. That's a good Star Trek episode right there. What could go wrong?

It turns out that we could go wrong. Our two-legged, ego-driven, independent-streaked, power-hungry, lust-led, pleasure-filled, thrill-seeking, insatiable, untrainable human prototype needed more.

I need more.

I'm as pure Protestant as you can get. "Give me that old time religion" could be my theme song: "it's good enough for me," says the refrain. Give me no creed, no hierarchy, no structure, no infringement. Just you, me and God in a little white clapboard church, that should do it.

Not entirely.

I find myself requiring help, looking for help, things to touch, words to say, some feast for my eyes. We each find that in our own way. I think that God long ago gave up on the idea that we would worship God as an unpronounceable, unimaginable, disembodied spirit. Besides, if the Garden of Eden represents the good old days of God/human relationships, those days were known for visual, audible, personal interaction. We don't need to shy away from it, as if such connection is beneath us. Not if the goal is connection.

Growing up in the simplicity of New England Congregational and Baptist leanings, bare and spare, I am new to ornate religious experience, and its power and

God as Opera

attraction. My first introduction, within Christianity, was at the over-the-top baroque Catholic Churches of Prague. Gigantic everything. Gilded altars with humongous saints slaying life-size dragons. Vaulted ceilings. Museum worthy art. Marble and columns and majesty.

Yet those who tell me they most clearly know God in a sunrise or sunset have no less a spectacle. Watching thousands of Muslim pilgrims, all dressed in white, all bent in the same posture and the same direction in prayer, that is mesmerizing. My daughter attended the world's largest Hindu festival, an every- six-year river immersion with twelve million Hindus.

At the same time, there are the quiet Quakers, the ecstatic Pentecostals, the formal Anglicans, the earnest Baptists, the simple Amish, the high church and low church and no church worshippers. Each finding in their own way a way that connects with God.

I recognize that the search for connection is very individual, and subject to the "grass is always greener." My few experiences of Orthodox Christianity (Greek and Serbian) have led me to kiss an icon on many occasions, each very moving and deeply spiritual. At least part of its power is that I've spent seven decades not kissing icons. If I had kissed an icon every Sunday my whole life, I am sure I would find visits to my austere, all white sanctuary very moving and deeply spiritual. Just like it is.

Against this background I found myself in a favorite, out of the way, non-tourist Catholic Church in Prague. It had been a productive day and week writing this book, both exhilarating and draining. Looking for a change of pace to re-charge my batteries, and for spiritual rest, I went to the Church of St. Thomas, a place familiar and friendly to me. When I do this, I look for an inconspicuous place to pray, a back pew, a side chapel, in part because I am there to pray, my prayer list is lengthy, I think of prayer as conversation with God, and so I tend to at least mumble and certainly move my lips, if not outright out loud. So, I isolate myself.

This day I used a kneeling bench before a painting of St. Rita. On the shelf-like top of the kneeling bench were two papers. One told me the life and ordeals and suffering of St. Rita. The other was a prayer to St. Rita, yes, to her. Not to God in general, not to Jesus for specifics. This was like an end-run or Plan C Prayer. You want God's attention, but you think you are not worthy, or God is too busy, or Jesus is too holy, or God is too remote. So, St. Rita is your back channel. By virtue of her saintly life, she has a uniquely intimate relationship with Jesus. What's more, the prayer highlights her life experiences and spiritual qualities that make her uniquely capable of carrying your (my) concerns to Jesus.

Okay. This is way out from my comfort zone. In my super Protestant world, prayer truly is a direct line from me to God, no intermediary, no thees and thous, no formula, and no Saint standing between me and God, ready to pass on my request.

But I did it.

I wish someone had a camera. There's me, this older, white-haired Protestant pastor, my cane leaning up against the kneeler, kneeling on my artificial knees. I put my iPhone on the kneeler shelf on the left-hand side, scroll down to my full prayer list of 45 church members and their specific needs, and I have the Prayer to St. Rita on the right-hand side. And then, semi out loud, I proceed to pray to St. Rita, glancing from left to right to match up my concerns with her unique capabilities.

Plus, it said I got three hundred days off of purgatory, for me or a loved one. So, I prayed it twice.

Trust me, I'm not mocking this. It's not my "thing" but I 100% felt this was a legitimate prayer, legitimately prayed on my end and legitimately received on God's end. It counted.

My Jesus opens the door to mysteries beyond my immediate comprehension. The Opera House in Paris certainly inspired me, intrigued me. It was spectacular. The sliced-in-half Opera House model opened up the spectacular to my understanding. I could now make sense of it all.

Jesus does that for me. And maybe St. Rita does that when an even more human connection seems helpful. Both make the love of God very real, very now, very personal.

Appendix (Printed exactly as found)

Prayer to St. Rita:

Let us pray.

O God, Who didst deign to confer on Saint Rita for imitating Thee in love of her enemies, the favor of bearing

My Jesus

on heart and brow the marks of Thy Love and Passion, grant, we beseech Thee, that through her intercession and merits, we may be pierced with the thorns of compunction, and ever contemplate the sufferings of Thy Passion, who livest and reignest for ever and ever.

Amen.

(Indulgence of 300 days for this prayer. Plenary indulgence under the usual conditions, if recited daily for a month. (No.567)

Supplication to St. Rita

Holy Patroness of those in need. Saint Rita, whose pleadings before thy Divine Lord are irresistible, who for thy lavishness in granting favors hast been called the "Advocate of the Hopeless," and even of the Impossible, Saint Rita, so humble, so pure, so mortified, so patient and of such compassionate love for thy Crucified Jesus, that thou canst obtain from Him anything thou dost ask, on account of which, all confidently have recourse to thee in the hope of comfort or relief; be propitious to thy suppliants and show thy power with God in their behalf; be lavish of thy favors now as thou hast been in so many wonderful cases for the greater glory of God, the spreading of thy devotion and the consolation of those who trust in thee. We promise, if our petition be granted, to glorify thee by making known thy favor, and to bless thee and sing thy praises forever. Relying then on thy merits and power before the Sacred Heart of Jesus, we ask of thee (Here mention your request.)

By the singular merits of thy childhood, By thy perfect union with the Divine Will, By thy heroic suffering during thy married life, By the consolation thou didst experience at the conversion of thy husband, By the anguish that filled thy heart at the murder of thy husband, By the sacrifice of thy children, rather than see them grievously offend God, By thy miraculous entrance into the convent, By thy severe penance and three times daily bloody scourging, By thy suffering from the wound received from the thorn of thy Crucified Saviour, By thy divine love which consumed thy heart, By thy remarkable devotion to the Blessed Sacrament, on which alone thou didst subsist for years, By the happiness with which thou didst part from thy trials to join thy Divine Spouse, Obtain our request for us.

NINE

What If I'm Wrong?

So, I die. Then I wake up, resurrected, whatever, glad to be alive again. Proud that everything I've preached at 1500 funerals is true!

Off in a distance I see people being welcomed, reunited, ushered in. That great city, The New Jerusalem, comes as advertised. Twelve gates, each made of a single pearl. Wow! How do they do that? Even at a distance the brightness is dazzling. You can see for yourself that the streets are paved with gold.

I did it. I lived my life to the best of my ability, I think. I was good, for the most part. Kept most of the commandments. At least I never killed anybody or built a graven image. I guess I have a pretty decent resume. I'm here, aren't I? The Book of Life is just ahead, open to the letter R.

I'm close enough now to see familiar faces, but first, believe it or not, there is some paperwork. But I'm not worried, really. I give St. Peter a hearty greeting, and Jesus the smile of an old friend.

They're not smiling. Or greeting. Or ushering me in.

Nearby, people are grumbling, frowning, pushing to the front but not getting anywhere. Something is awry.

What's he saying? one person asks, looking troubled. *What's the hold up? I had a reservation,* one yells. *I paid for this,* grumbles another. *Nobody's gonna tell me where to go, I worked hard for this. Do they know who I am? Who do they think they are, for Chrissake?* The epithets are growing.

After a while, exhaustion sets in.

Dying can take a lot out of you, physically and emotionally. So drawn out. Everyone overwrought. Indecision about whether it is time to let go, or fight on. Goodbyes. Not so goodbyes. Guilt. People whispering, *okay, you can let go now, we'll be fine.* The living are trying to be helpful. The dying are trying not to be a burden. It is an exhausting journey.

The upside, for those of us in this clump of unhappy resurrectees, is supposed to be this: here, heaven, the kingdom of God, Paradise.

Peter, a big burly guy, seems to be in charge. Now he starts barking orders, answering questions, shouting explanations all at once.

"You, over here!"

"You, there. No, not there. There!" And he points down south.

I catch bits and pieces that begin to explain the delay, if that's what it is. Obviously, some misunderstandings. Also, ominous. People are talking about sheep and goats, weeping and gnashing of teeth, outer darkness. Most troubling happens right near, a woman crying out, "Lord, Lord," beseeching, begging. And Jesus, very simply and very clearly looks at her. "I don't know you," he says.

My Jesus

Whatever is about to happen, that moment captures it all. Maybe I've been wrong.

A little melodramatic, perhaps, this chapter opening.

Having been a pastor a long time, I've garnered my share of critics. People have left my church over female ushers and helping to settle refugees, over blessing gay couples and promoting missionary work, over too much Jesus and not enough blood.

The truly earnest ones were concerned about eternity. If eternity is real and forever, a pastor's job must be to steer people in a way that ends them up on the right side of eternity.

Visiting my grandfather late in his life, I saw him staring into the distance. "What are you thinking about, Grandpa?" I asked, hoping for some family memory, pastoral tidbit, historical reference, or Biblical insight I could carry with me after he was gone.

"Eternity," was his answer. "What else is there?"

The Bible agrees. This life, even for the healthiest among us, is all too brief. We are "soon cut off and we fly away" (Psalm 90:10) ... "our days are a shadow that passeth away" (Psalm 144:4) ... "we are but flesh, a wind that passes and does not return" (Psalm 78:39) ... "just a vapor that appears for a little while and then vanishes" (James 4:14). All true, even for the best and most long-lived among us. The clincher verse is this: "it is appointed to us once to die, but after this the judgement" (Hebrews 9:27).

There you go: death, then eternity.

What If I'm Wrong?

Christians debate and vary widely about what happens after death. The good, the righteous, the saved, the born again, the ones whose names are written in the Book of Life live forever with an exquisite joy. The others face a punishment that is equally long. They get raised, judged and tormented forever. The Catholics add purgatory, a place of middling punishment to purge us of our sins before finally getting heaven. Forever.

Or heaven is for everyone, or there isn't one. Whether there's something or nothing, eternity is still forever, and that is a long time.

So, of course, I wonder. Have I led my people astray? I've bet my own life on a certain outcome. What's more, as a pastor, I've led tens of thousands to expect a certain outcome.

"God is so good. God is so good. God is so good, he's so good to me," I taught generations of Sunday School children to sing. "Amazing Grace, how sweet the sound that saved a wretch like me," has been sung at countless funerals, sending loved ones on their blessed way no matter their track record. God's love is greater, I have assured thousands and thousands of people, greater than their loss, their failure, their regrets, their sins; greater than death itself. If there is one thing we can count on it is God's love, through Christ, winning for eternity. I preach, teach and believe that.

The Jesus part of the Bible is not Johnny One Note. I play it like a mostly one note, and that note is very reassuring. But is it the wrong note? Or a half-note? My note is Love. Love again. Love some more. Keep at it. It is all there in the "red letter" scriptures by Jesus and in the black letter scriptures about Jesus. Love: do it, be it, repeat it.

Popular music and pop culture kick in with the same refrain. "Love is all you need," the Beatles sang, as if on endless loop. "Love makes the world go 'round," O. Henry wrote, no doubt plagiarizing a thousand others. Even cynics have their take, from "Love hurts" to "Love stinks" to the more hopeful "'Tis better to have loved and lost than never to have loved at all."

Prioritizing love is well travelled territory, even theologically. That does not guarantee it is always well received.

The four harshest letters and personal condemnations I have received all took issue with my pastoral and preaching emphasis on God's undying love. Criticism is fair game but what got me was their suggestion that love is the easy path, the easy teaching, the lazy way out of dealing with God's dark side.

Now that's a stretch.

The Bible tells us to "love God with all our hearts, with all our soul and with all our mind" (Matthew 22:37), plus "love your neighbor as yourself" (Matthew 22:39), plus "love your enemies" (Matthew 5:44 – and yes, plural), plus several varieties of loving the stranger and the foreigner, all wrapped up in Jesus' bold declaration: "A new commandment I give you: Love one another; as I have loved you, love one another" (John 13:34).

What If I'm Wrong?

That seems clear as day. That seems pretty big. That seems high priority. Maybe the priority.

And none of that seems easy. We can love people who love us. And people who are like us. People who agree with us. People who are plain loveable. Our pets and kids and teammates. Heroes and celebrities and leaders, if we don't know them too well.

However, the Bible's list of love is bolder. Everybody. I would challenge anyone to compile their own list, a personal list, of who is unlovable, or unworthy of your love, or at the least is tough to love. Don't start with Hitler: that is a cop-out. Make your own personal list of people you cannot love.

Then, imagine what it would take to love them. That should end the criticism that choosing a theology of love is the lazy way out. What's more, the Christian's urgency to love is rooted in the horrific end of Jesus' human life on the cross. Easy? For whom?

And yet it is true that, for all the evidence of God's love, of love as the overarching theme of Jesus' life, his very raison d'être, there are compelling verses that are way more than cautionary. They can act as an addendum to 1 John 4:8, 16 so that it would read "God is love. Yes, but ..."

Early on in his ministry, Jesus declared "I have not come to abolish the Law, but to fulfill it," promising not to change a "jot or tittle of the Law" (Matthew 5:17-18). He then proceeded to toughen well-known, well-agreed upon laws such as adultery and murder by condemning lust and anger as the true crimes.

My Jesus

For someone who was not going to change jot or tittle, he does exactly that. Jesus took a favorite Bible verse of so many, "an eye for an eye, a tooth for a tooth" (Leviticus 24:19-21) and wipes it from the Bible as clearly as Thomas Jefferson with his scissors. "I say unto you, do not resist the one who is evil. But if anyone slaps you on the right cheek, turn to him the other also" (Matthew 5:38-39). Jesus may not say it straight out right there, but it feels like he is setting the stage for the primacy of love and all that is loving.

Still, Jesus offers plenty of consequences with implications for eternity. He mentions "weeping and gnashing of teeth" often enough that it should get our attention, make us think.

I don't like to fire people. But I have used the word "fire" as a wakeup call for those willing to wake up. The conversation usually goes, "Hi, Joe, glad you came in. Have a seat. Now, this meeting isn't to fire you." Then I ramble on from work habits to sports to work habits to family. But Joe learned that firing is in my vocabulary.

Jesus lets us know that an eternity of "weeping and gnashing" is in his vocabulary, among his options. Those options are within his rights. Starting with the concept of God, branching out to Judge and King and Lord, there is the right to punish people eternally in such a way that "weeping and gnashing of teeth" are the only sounds.

The starkest reminder is the famous passage of "the sheep and the goats" (Matthew 25:31-46). Very bluntly Jesus lays out two eternities. For those who "do unto the least as fully as they would do unto (Jesus himself)" there is a "Kingdom prepared for you since the creation of the world" (Matthew 25:34). For those who refuse to see Jesus in the very presence of others in need he says, "Depart from me, you who are cursed, into the eternal fire prepared for the devil and his angels" (vs. 41). For both groups, the result is "eternal" (vs. 46).

Not to rush by the punishment aspect, but it is worth noting that eternal damnation and eternal life are not predicated on doctrine. Only on loving.

The nature of that damnation punishment has intrigued humanity always. In Christian circles, much of our thinking about Hell comes from Dante's *Inferno*. Gruesome, endless, specific, ironic and exquisite tortures perfectly match what got the sinner into Inferno in the first place.

But for a Bible as thick as ours, and a topic that has consumed our imagination, there is precious little about heaven or hell in the scriptures. When my mother died my father began an exhaustive study, wanting to know what my mother was experiencing and what awaited him. He found there was a generalized, overall picture of heaven and hell: the one a place to sacrifice anything for, the other a place to be avoided at all costs. There are a few comforting and disturbing descriptions, like no marriage and no tears. The "when" is left fuzzier and accommodates the two opposite ends: Judgement Day at the end of time for everyone all at once, or Paradise "this day", as Jesus promised to the Good Thief on the cross (Luke 23:43).

My Jesus

The Parable of the Rich Man and Lazarus (Luke 16:19-31) puts eternity in the most human terms. Both men die and begin their separate eternities. Lazarus, a beggar, who had lived his life at the Rich Man's gate, eating scraps from the table, ends up in a pleasant place of great honor. He's fine.

The Rich Man ends up in a place that is characterized as "torment," very hot, exceedingly dry, with an imposing but visible divide between the two. He's not fine.

Once again, we have God exercising Godly justice, as is God's right. The Rich Man had both a lifetime and the resources to do the right thing by his neighbor. He failed. As the saying goes, "he did the crime, now he has to do the time." And the time is an eternity of torment.

There are more such verses. There is no need to cherry-pick verses to support the emphasis on God's love nor cherry-pick verses that emphasize God's righteous judgement. They are all in The Good Book.

In the last week of his life Jesus travels to Jerusalem, stops at a fig tree hoping for a quick energy boost, only to find the tree barren. The Bible makes it clear that it is not even the season for figs (Mark 11:12-14; 20-25). Yet Jesus curses the fig tree, and when they return later the poor fig tree is withered, dead.

Gee, whiz. No one has ever turned that Bible story into a hymn, or a great work of art. Yet there it is. Jesus uses this head-scratcher to offer two lessons about the power of faith to move mountains and to forgive. But the killing of the fig tree parallels a similar teaching, that we are expected to bear fruit (John 15:1-2, 5-6). No excuses like, hey, it's not the season for figs.

These warnings of God's righteous indignation are there from one end of the Bible to other, and I don't underestimate them. As an obstinate child, a veteran parent and grandparent, a longtime coach, a lifetime teacher, and as a careerlong church pastor I know the frustrations that give way to anger. I want the best for someone, and they won't listen, won't try. Righteous anger and righteous indignation are not strong enough. Righteous rage is more like it.

If we admit that in ourselves, we can easily see that in God, whose own perfection and demands for perfection ("be ye perfect," Matthew 5:48) would make the brightest and the best cower. God has the right to rage.

Lots of people love the smell of hellfire and brimstone. It keeps them on the straight and narrow. It fuels their zeal to save others. Or it satisfies their lust for holier than thou self-righteousness. I've been on the receiving end of the full range of eternal damnation motivation. My grandfather's true belief in The Lake of Fire caused his earnest prayer for my salvation, at the point when there was not a hint in me of anything worth saving. That is the power of eternity, subject to God's toughest standard, that I respect.

On the odious end of the damnation spectrum was a religious cult that tried to insert itself in our church life. Starting friendly enough, two men joined our Bible Study. Eventually, their purpose was made clear. They had a message for our church and wanted to take over our

My Jesus

Bible Study and worship pulpit to deliver that message. To wit, the Second Coming of Jesus had already happened in the person of their cult leader. And this second version of Jesus was "no more Mr. Nice Guy. This time he's pissed." All that love, love, love stuff of 30 A.D. had only gotten the first Jesus killed. And had failed miserably in the 2000 years since. Now he's not fooling around. Follow this Jesus Plan B or spend eternity in hell. The wimpy Jesus is over.

That was their sales pitch to lead our church. Standing on the front lawn, after I refused them, they pronounced a curse on me, our church, and all our people. Rather happily, it seemed.

In a nutshell, my grandfather hated hell and wanted me in heaven. The cult guys loved hell and wanted me there. Their "go to hell" stands in stark contrast to my grandfather's living bumper sticker, "God loves you and there's absolutely nothing you can do about it." To which I say, *thank God.*

My point is, God is God. Whether it is the God of the Three O's (omnipotent, omnipresent, omniscient) or my "What a Friend We Have in Jesus," God is still God. As such, God has every right to judge this earth and all its occupants to the full extent of the Law.

The Bible certainly does say "All have sinned and fall short of the glory of God" (Romans 3:23), and does warn "the penalty of sin is death" (Romans 6:23), and does describe the ultimate end of humanity's worst as "the lake that burns with fire and sulfur, which is the second death" (Revelation 21:8).

What If I'm Wrong?

The question, the eternal question, is whether God would pull the trigger on that theological nuclear option? Is the nature of God so perfect and just that God cannot abide any sin or sinner in his midst? Or is the nature of God so perfectly revealed in Jesus that they cannot abide the loss of even one sheep, one coin, one prodigal son (Luke 15)?

We are all Hall of Fame Christians. Bear with this analogy. A really good baseball player hits .300. If you hit .300 in Little League and Babe Ruth League you will make your high school team. Hit .300 in high school you have a chance to play at college. A .300 college hitter might well play professional ball. And if that player keeps hitting .300 there will be a place for them in the Hall of Fame, secured for eternity. Note that .300 represents 30%. A great baseball player successfully hits the ball thirty percent of the time and is unsuccessful seventy percent of the time.

That is most of us, spiritually. The spiritual superstars we know or admire may "hit" for a higher average, but even they "fall short of the glory of God," and God's perfection.

What damnation awaits the best of us, and the worst? The torturous imaginings of Dante? The lake that burns with fire and sulfur? Enough to make us pray to St. Rita a whole lot? Or do we all get to use that "get out of jail free" card hidden in our Monopoly game?

Jesus warns that we should "enter by the narrow gate; for wide is the gate and broad is the way that leads to destruction ... but narrow is the gate and difficult is the

My Jesus

way that leads to life" (Matthew 7: 13-14). Even more distressingly, Jesus adds "and there are few who find it." Some translations have it, "narrow is the way."

No matter what, it is tough going. Whether it is Jesus telling us to "pick up our cross and follow him" (Luke 9:23), or the whole Sermon on the Mount with its nigh unto impossible standards, all the way to the demanding and specific calls to love – yes, the way is exceedingly narrow.

Our flimsy hope is encouraged by a fascinating conversation in Matthew 19. There is a lot of back and forth about who is good, and how to get to heaven, with even Jesus' followers getting increasingly pessimistic. "Who then can be saved?" they asked aloud (Matthew 19:25).

I get that. When I consider the list of people I've been told are not saved it rules out a good 80-90% of Americans. Gay people, Jews, divorced people, Hindus and Muslims, people not baptized or who don't speak in tongues, Democrats, liberals, Catholics, people who drink or dance or have life insurance. Who then can be saved, indeed?

Yet Jesus stunningly ends such theological finger pointing by saying, "with God all things are possible" (Matthew 19:26).

I am not denying the narrowness of the way or the gate. I am objecting to the narrowness of the mind that consigns God's children to eternal oblivion. It doesn't jibe with the Jesus given to us, nor with the sacrifice Jesus made.

What If I'm Wrong?

Narrow is the way that made my father happy. That was learned at an early age. Play baseball March-August. Get two hits a game and throw out runners. The rest of the year, sweat somehow. When not sweating, read. Then read some more. Get to church on time. Linger after, help out. Do all that and you have a reasonable chance of eating dinner in peace.

That is a fairly narrow path leading to a narrow gate.

But failure to do so, to adjust to the structures of his domain, did not lead to death, banishment, shunning, violence.

One could make the argument that it led to purgatory, I'll grant you that. Purgatory was mostly extra baseball practice, more reading, and legendary lectures that could last an eternity.

I mention this family story because one of the essential and unique contributions of Jesus to worldwide theology is the idea of intimacy with God. We are God's children, invited to call God "Father" and "Daddy," seeing in God both maternal and paternal instincts, and in line to be God's inheritors. That is not liberal claptrap. That is Jesus telling us about his relationship with his father, offering us the same. We are family.

Some Christians have experienced confidence in God's universal salvation from earliest times. At its worst it is mocked as "anything goes ... if it feels good, do it," no consequences, family hug. God as marshmallow.

At its best, it is a humble recognition that God's greatness is greater than anything we can imagine, God's

My Jesus

grace is greater than anything we have experienced, God's love is greater than anything we can deserve.

Such thinking results in two immediate responses. First, the ever popular "What about Hitler?" I can't let the unmatchable horror of Hitler blind me to God's truest essence. As written earlier, what God does with Hitler is God's business. My calling is to describe the truth of God's love in Christ as fully as possible.

The second response is, if there is no hell or purgatory or damnation, why should anyone be good? Aside from the inherent cynicism of the question, or at least a cynical view of life, it is a fair question. So, we all do what we want, and God is fine with that just because we are God's kids?

No, God is not fine with that. But I can imagine a reckoning that does not involve exquisite or eternal torture, or smell like sulfur, or hurt like hell. I choose the word "imagine" purposefully. The Book of Revelation, our go-to Biblical book for descriptions of eternity, requires imagination. Its bottom line is that heaven is beyond spectacular. And to miss it would be a loss beyond measure.

With that invitation to imagination, I put the Jesus of my experience and the Jesus of the Gospels to work. Like my own father, Jesus has lectured us, has worked us extra hard, has raised the bar way high, has narrowed the path, and has used every motivational tool to get us on the right track.

As for punishment, I turn to my mother. My mother never raised her voice or her hand, never meted out a single punishment, never offered a cross word or harsh judgement, never made a threat.

However, she was not a pushover, or oblivious, or without feeling. That feeling came through in her look. The look. At whatever latest failure I presented, there was The Look of Disappointment. Bad report card, caught smoking or in a lie, any and all of my teenage rebellion, each sin was met by her Look of Disappointment. Whatever teenage good I accomplished was an attempt to avoid that look.

In my short story "Jesus at Auschwitz" (from *Water Into Wine*) I imagine the eternal life punishment of the ISIS terrorist who beheaded James Foley, the innocent American journalist. In the story, as I wander Auschwitz with Jesus, I pepper and attack him with angry questions. At some point, to impress upon me the extraordinary depth of his own wounded love, Jesus informs me that Foley's murderer is with him in heaven. I am disgusted beyond belief, and you read that phrase correctly. By way of explanation, and adding to the mystery of salvation, Jesus tells me the terrorist wears a burqa "because he's afraid to meet his mother," embarrassed by the depths of his depravity.

With the limits of my human understanding and the gift of imagination, and the memories of personal experience, I can believe that, despite our worst, God's welcome embrace touches us with a look powerful enough to singe our soul, close the wound, and heal us for all eternity. Heaven and hell, both real. One stronger than the other. One forever.

TEN

The End

> The end is work.
> The work is love.
> The love is resurrection.
> The resurrection is love.
> The love is work.
> The work is the end.

I have had a supernatural experience, several of them. A voice, a vision, an intervention, a miracle, grace, power – all from an outside source, incontrovertibly real. Individually and collectively, they confirm the otherwise unconfirmable: the resurrection of Jesus from the dead. That supernatural event gives life and breath to all the supernatural events that form the Christian experience.

Our final chapter will include more of Tomáš Halík. In an interview on ABC Television's "Religion and Ethics," Halík quoted a story by his "favorite theologian," Nicholas Lash of Cambridge University. Lash says that if you come across a rabbit playing Mozart on the violin you can bet your bottom dollar that the rabbit is acting supernaturally. It is not in a rabbit's nature to play the violin, much less Mozart. Likewise, given humankind's propensity for greed, violence, selfishness and the like, if we come across human beings acting with consistent kindness, selflessness, generosity, grace and the like, we can assume a supernatural influence, a force at work (from an interview with Frank Brennan, ABC Religion and Ethics, May 9, 2012, quoting Nicholas Lash from *Holiness, Speech and Silence*).

That force is the resurrected Jesus resurrected in us as evidenced by a continually resurrecting life of faith.

You have made it through an abundance of pages devoted to what I believe and know and trust about Jesus. Ample room is even given to rebuttal, to the possibility that I am wrong, knowing full well that half of Christianity and half of my deeply committed Christian friends and loved ones will disagree.

A person once challenged me, asking "If I can prove with absolute certainty that there is no God, will you stop praying?" "No," I assured him. Whatever absolute certainty he could conjure would run up against my reality, the only reality I know. That must include the reality of God known to me in the presence and person and voice and intervention and words and life of the very Jesus whom I claim as mine. Not mine alone, but mine in full.

St. Paul faced a similar quandary when, after viciously terrorizing those early Christians before his conversion, he suddenly shows up at their front door proclaiming the Christ who personally took hold of him. Peter and others of the original, first-person followers of Jesus were skeptical of this latecomer who claimed his own in-person experience of the resurrected Christ equal to their in-the-flesh relationship. All this is in Acts 9:1-26. Paul bet his life and career, as I do, on a personal relationship that is real, vital, and tangible in its own way.

My Jesus

The writing of this book began in sidewalk cafes of summer lit Paris, when all was well. The second half was written, and all the correcting and editing done, during the Annus Horribilis, the horrible year of 2020. Together we endured the pandemic shutdown, the incoherent response, the merciless murders of Black citizens, the urgent protests and calls for reform, and the enraged riots whose destruction mirrored the brokenness of people and promises.

Halík incessantly asks Jesus-followers if we are aware of the "signs of the times." His unplanned mentorship of me began with his book, *Patience with God*. There followed more books, many private conversations, the Duffy Lectures at Boston College, along with sermons and lectures he would send to me. This Halík Library concentrates on four themes: the radical love of God to which we are called; the wounds of Christ so evident all around to anyone with half a heart; the requirement of any church worth the name to read and respond to "the signs of the times"; and the urgency to be proof of resurrection in all our ministry.

These times range from a virulent virus to absurdist politics to racial conflict to economic uncertainty – a smorgasbord of chaos that is resistant and resilient.

Our church is approaching its 300th Anniversary. Some of our history is researchable and knowable. But the most interesting aspects are lost. Over those three hundred years, how did this church read and respond to the signs of their times? Beginning in 1725, the Christians of Greenfield Hill Congregational Church were certainly

The End

immersed in the growing revolutionary fervor leading up to independence, the anti-slavery movement significantly birthed in Connecticut, the ensuing Civil War, the struggle for the vast array of human rights, the deprivations of the Depression, the tragic costs of World Wars and partial wars – where were the people of our church? What preaching and teaching guided them? How did their commitment to the resurrected Christ impact and inform their opinions, actions?

We don't know. At best it is known that they endured their times and bequeathed to us a place of faithful worship.

While we may not recover those times, we are responsible for how we face the signs of our times.

The saddest conversation with my father concerned his marching with Dr. Martin Luther King, Junior from Selma to Montgomery. The initial walk began with a bloody bashing of marchers on the infamous Edmund Pettus Bridge. Dr. King issued a call to clergy to join the second attempt, and my father answered that call. Years later I asked him how his church reacted to his participation in the famous march.

"I never told them," he told me, "I was not certain of their reaction." In other words, my father responded justly and prophetically to the signs of the times, a response that grew even deeper over time. But his church, like many, missed the signs and stayed sidelined.

To meet the signs of any times is to be so immersed in resurrection that it rubs off on us, it becomes us. We

My Jesus

are not inert, unresponsive, without feeling, finished or dead to the world. To be immersed in resurrection is to be so full of "convincing proofs" (Acts 1:3) that the observing world will be stunned by our commitment to loving, as they were in the early days of the Church. That stunning reputation took Christianity from humble beginnings to center stage. After centuries on center stage, it may be best, even God's will, that we return to being stunning and humble.

Halík again, from his seminal *Dotkni se ran (Touch the Wounds):*

> The message of the resurrection means above all that God acknowledges Christ crucified whom people rejected: 'the stone that the builders rejected has become the cornerstone' (Psalm 118:22).
>
> God heard the dying cry of his Son, to which people turned a deaf ear and from which the apostles fled in fear. And what is more, through the cry of His Son, through His cross and death, He hears the cry of all victims in countless nights of our history. 'History is written by the victors' (it is said) – but God hears the victims. (Resurrection means) God does not permit their lives to tumble into the darkness of nothingness and absurdity. However powerful they may now seem, death, violence and injustice will not have the last word. That is also – and maybe chiefly – the meaning of the message of the resurrection.

(Excerpts from Selected Books for the Templeton Prize, First Chapter of *Dotkni se ran, Touch the Wounds,* Prague 2008)

Or, as he said in his Duffy Lectures, "Jesus is the ongoing event of God's encounter with humanity ... Jesus' victory over death continues in personal stories and in the historical stories of the Church – a subterranean river that emerges and brings light and life to our darkness" (Duffy Lectures, Boston College, 2020).

In other words, God did something on Easter with Jesus that softens and silences all the death rattles of our lives and of history. Our responsibility, then, is to do something with our resurrection faith that will continue to soften and silence the death rattles of our times.

If Jesus is the stand-in for all the wounds of history and of our times, then it is urgent to ask, where are the Church and Church people in such a world of woundedness?

In my book *Church: One Pilgrim's Progress* I recall an overwhelming faith experience in the Cathedral of Guatemala City.

Near the entrance, to the left of the main Nave, separate from the side chapels, stood a life-size, bloodied Jesus hanging on the cross. Both shocked and quite taken, I observed the scene at a safe distance as people approached the cross. One at a time they climbed a wooden step, bowed their heads, spoke silent prayers and wept. Then they leaned forward, embraced the body of their Jesus and began to caress Jesus' legs, as if they

My Jesus

could take away some of his pain. As a final act of devotion, they bent down and kissed the feet of Jesus.

After too much struggle with my Protestant upbringing, I finally joined the line, soon to find myself face to face with the wounds of Jesus. And I, too, wept, caressing his legs, kissing his feet, feeling his pain.

Can we make such devotion real in daily life, not just in private?

May I insert two bird stories? Despite being an inveterate squirrel lover, birds still fascinate me and, thankfully, our birds and squirrels abide harmoniously.

On the campus of nearby Fairfield University is a statue of St. Kevin, one hand up in the air holding a bird's nest. Titled "St. Kevin and the Blackbirds," it tells in stone the story of St. Kevin. Having found a nest of baby blackbirds orphaned from care, he held his arm aloft, holding the nest and the little birds in his hand, as if a sturdy tree branch. There they remained until able to fly and prosper.

Yet again from the world of birds, this story. It is reported frantically, "the sky is falling, the sky is falling, the end is near!!" Everyone is panicked and afraid, scurrying hither and yon, accomplishing nothing. It is further reported that a little bird is lying on its back in the village square with its tiny legs and arms arched up toward the heavens. Everyone wants to know, with a mocking and dismissive tone, what the bird is doing? "Don't you know how silly you look? With your scrawny legs twisting in the air, what can you possibly do?", more a taunt than a question.

The End

"One does what one can," states the little bird, with surprising confidence.

In each bird story life is affirmed over death, Easter faith over Good Friday fact, resurrection over crucifixion. They do not deny the reality of death, Good Friday or crucifixions, nor do I. Instead, we choose a life of faith focused on all that is hopeful. We focus on resurrection living.

There are two phrases that stopped me dead in my tracks and transformed my ministry. The first is "Christlikeness." My dear Indian partner in mission, K. Azariah, used the word in Bible study and it was an instant epiphany, a theological "aha" moment when the light really did go on and I could see clearly the task of church and pastor. Until that moment I had spent my career trying to create little Protestants of one denomination or another. Success was measured by having more on December 31 than I had on January 1, more members and baptisms and confirmations.

Christlikeness is an entirely different goal, harder to count but truer to the source. We are to be as much like Christ as possible. And when we fall short, we get up the next day, shake off our failure, and try harder. Indeed, this book totally devoted to Jesus is devoted to Christlikeness.

The second theological word play that grabbed my attention is "Resurrecto Continuo." In Halík's Duffy Lectures, during the question-and-answer period after and in private conversations, he repeatedly returned to this Latin phrase for "continuing resurrection." His point was that contemporary Christianity cannot be satisfied (or satisfying) only pointing towards the occasion of Jesus' resurrection on that first Easter two thousand years ago. We must be engaged in continuing resurrection, ongoing resurrection, lots of resurrections. We can prove God's ability and willingness, and ours, to continually breathe new life into people and places and needs that had been given up for dead or dismissed as decrepit or beyond repair. From individual hope to inner cities, from the sick to the elderly, from dying churches to broken relationships, from timeless conflicts to daily depression – we are the bearers and doers of resurrecto continuo.

Our strongest convincing testimony to Christ is our convincing proof of continuous resurrections resulting from our Christlikeness. There, that's the two in one: Christlikeness and continuous resurrections. Do both.

It is not up to Jesus to convince us that He is living within and among and through us. He exists, whether we are convinced and convincing, or not. Nor is it up to you or me to convince each other that we exist. You, me and God can all claim, "I am that I am."

Nevertheless, the world beyond absolute faith seeks assurance. We are all, for the most part, theological residents of Missouri – the "show me" state. St. Thomas, before being a Saint, bluntly declared that he would not believe in Jesus' resurrection until he could personally verify the very wounds in Jesus' hands and side and feet (John 20:25).

The End

Even Jesus understood the necessity of providing enough "convincing proofs" to the first generation of believers that their faith would be unshakeable.

But what will make today's faith unshakeable?

Like the Guatemala City worshippers embracing Jesus on the cross, Halík pushes us to find the wounds of life and embrace them. During a visit with Fr. Halík after Mass in his Prague church, he told me a story about St. Mark. The devil visited Mark, hoping to undermine his faith by coming disguised as Jesus. It was a convincing disguise. The robe, the sandals, the voice and demeanor all accurately portrayed the Jesus of Mark's love. But one thing was missing: the wounds in Jesus' hands and feet and side. Mark knew that a Christ without wounds is not Christ. The devil was unmasked by his avoidance of wounds. Our Christlikeness is proven by our proximity with, and embrace of, wounds.

What convincing proofs have deepened our faith? And what do we offer as convincing proofs to others in search of faith? To have any power our lived faith today must have a direct connection to that original Easter day when, from sunup to sundown, it was increasingly and personally clear that resurrection was the order of the day. Fact, not hope or rumor. Real.

One of the most ongoing political debates of our time is over whether the United States Constitution is a "living" document, subject to interpretation in light of the times. Or should we adhere to "originalist" thinking, that it was perfect in its origins and does not need tampering or broadening? Does it speak to us today other than what

My Jesus

was written then? In my lifetime LGBTQ people, people of color, the elderly, the disabled, Native Americans and women have found liberation and affirmation in an ancient document that never touched upon such a breadth of people. Yet because of what was stated as truth way back when, people have taken that truth to new levels.

It is the joy of contemporary Christianity in every age that ancient Easter can resonate in modern resurrections – the joy and the challenge.

Certainly, during this writing, the challenge of the Covid 19 pandemic awoke us to nature, itself, groaning under the weight of human choices. In addition, racism and its partner isms continue to challenge our very idea of human exceptionalism. These wounds and others, as signs of our times, beg the convincing proof of our resurrection faith. If we are unable, or worse, unwilling, to meet such challenges, why should anyone even try to believe our incredible story of Jesus' resurrection?

A recent image grabbed my attention. We were walking through Boston's famous North End, the great Italian neighborhood built along the Freedom Trail which celebrates the events of the Revolutionary War. You know: Bunker Hill, Paul Revere, Crispus Attucks.

Down the street came a strong, young Black man, dressed all in black. In one of the whitest parts of one of the Northeast's whitest cities with one of the most troubled Black/White histories, this fellow stood out. In a move clearly designed to make even the brain-dead

The End

think twice, his t-shirt carried the message "Don't Tread on Me."

Interesting. Provocative. Historical. Patriotic. And wonderfully ironic.

It was the Tea Party, enraged by Obama's presidency, that resurrected the pre-Revolutionary War battle flag for freedom with its threatening slogan, "Don't Tread on Me." The Tea Party's mixture of tri-corner hats, camouflage outfits and Confederate flags, more guns and less taxes, no regulations and no Obama had a chilling and humorous effect.

Two hundred and fifty years earlier, New Englanders waved that flag at British soldiers and officialdom, with the warning spectra of a coiled snake, in pursuit of liberty and justice.

The double irony of a Black man claiming that patriotic motto for himself – "Don't Tread on Me" – in the weeks following George Floyd's murder by a policeman who treaded on his neck for nine deadly minutes, is powerful. We are not alone in loving our country. We are not alone in demanding justice. We are not alone in resurrecting the best in each of us and each other.

These are our times, yearning, as all times do, for the resurrection proofs first provided by Jesus' Easter.

As mentioned in Chapter Two, we befriended a fascinating group of young Christians from Bratislava. Their nation had been fifty years under the anti-Christ of

My Jesus

the Nazis and then behind the Iron Curtain of communism.

Yet they were vibrant in their faith, dedicated to Christ, deeply committed to Church, proudly evangelistic. So, we talked at length about Jesus. Why is Jesus important? What is the message of Jesus for today, right now? With so many people nowadays against religion or church who are atheist or angry or hurt, what do you tell them about Jesus? And who is Jesus to you?

Each question built on the one before, the conversation growing and expanding. They recognized that their fervent Christian faith was a surprise to classmates, co-workers, friends, even family. Involved in Church, going to Mass not just on Sundays, travelling to see the Pope, using Christ as the guide for daily life, choosing a morality out of sync with 21st Century western culture put them in a position of extraordinary witness. They welcomed it.

In a joyful torrent of comment, they told us, "In our world we can see what is happening without Jesus. When people see us, they should see what is happening with Jesus. You know the song "They'll know we are Christians by our love." It should show. People always ask us why we are calm and optimistic, and where we get our energy from? It is easy to tell them what we get from our faith, because they see it. People have an empty space; they want to fill it with something. They can see how we are filled from God and from our faith and from Christian friends."

The End

They didn't take a breath as their love for Jesus poured out of them, and I was breathless listening to them.

"These are very important questions," they stated several times, explaining their zeal to answer. "I can do nothing alone," one said, as others nodded vigorously. "But," added another, "with Jesus I am never alone. I need to be transformed and to transform others. If people see the connection between the presenter of Christ and their own life then people will want to listen, and to know."

We were eating at an Italian restaurant outside of Bratislava, commandeering a long table with priests at both ends, Alida and I in the middle, the young people surrounding us. The energy around the table was electric, each person leaning in, intent, all taking turns to enter the conversation. It was that important.

One by one they affirmed that "the number one message of Christ is forgiveness. And there is a depth to the forgiveness that comes only from Christ." One explained, "on a human level, person to person, there may be forgiveness. But something will still be missing. Maybe resentment is still there. We hold on to bad feelings. But the forgiveness of Christ is true and complete. It is the only model for us of such forgiveness."

I remarked that I was quite surprised to see so many young adults at daily evening Mass. Again, they emphasized that being together in church is the real antidote to the loneliness and confusion of life that everyone is feeling. "Especially the services of reconciliation, then we have the real experience of forgiveness. We see clearly the importance of forgiving yourself, which is possible when it is backed up by all Jesus did, and does, for our forgiveness. We can forgive ourselves; we can believe it. That's what we mean by the depth of forgiveness. That's why it is good to see the arm and hand holding the cross, sticking out from the pulpit."

These are the priests and the young people who grew up in the two generations after the fall of Communism. Whatever Lenin and Stalin and Brezhnev thought they were accomplishing in decades of terror against faith was unravelling.

"We know society watches us, our friends, too, to see if our faith is real. It is Jesus who makes the essentials of faith and God and church real. It is us who make Jesus real, people willing to take Jesus seriously. Christianity has done much damage to Christ in the past. It is up to us to be the Jesus of love and truth in the present. He is the lighthouse and beacon for us, and we must be that, also."

The weight of this importance was felt around the table. And then the weight was lifted when one of the students smiled fully and added, "It is a joy when people look at us. It is a joy when we look to Him."

We come now to the end. And the end is work. And the work is love. Which is not as easy as it should be.

Being a workaholic who wrote a book about work, growing up in a family that revered work as the fulfillment of every person's calling, who went to a boarding school that required work every day not to cut costs but to build character, who worked the most menial

The End

jobs through Prep School and College, who signed up for three jobs in seminary, where family will attest that I work an awful lot on vacation, and who can't wait to start each day of work, it will come as no surprise that "The End" is work. Not Jesus' resurrection.

The resurrection would seem a perfect ending. I not only love it but believe every detail of it. I believe that several women went to the tomb, that they were first shocked and then convinced, that Mary Magdalene spoke personally with Jesus; that the male disciples were mocking and dismissive, disbelieving. I believe that Peter and John did check out the tomb and found nothing, that the discouraged men on the road to Emmaus were shocked into faith when the Risen Christ revealed Himself at their dinner table, and that Jesus stunned his closest friends by visiting with them that first Easter night. That was a great ending.

But it was not Jesus' ending. For Jesus, the totally astounding resurrection was really a prelude. He spent the next few weeks working, being out and among and with people, talking and teaching and doing. These were the accumulation of "convincing proofs" that created Christian faith. In a somewhat humorous end to this ending Luke, writing in Acts, tells us about Jesus' ascension "up into the sky" at which point two angels ask the Disciples, "why do you stand here looking into the sky?" (Acts 1)

That gentle reprimand was a call to work, to action. Indeed, Luke's account is called The Acts of the Apostles: Acts, as in action, work, doing. The end of Jesus' earthly

My Jesus

story is the inauguration of our work. Just as with Alec McGowan in his Broadway presentation of The Gospel of Mark, it is time to roll up our sleeves and get to work. And the work is love. And the love is resurrection.

In Conclusion

Are we an upper room foretaste of the eschatology?
(Tomáš Halík)

Closing arguments, last words, final thoughts are always in search of the perfect turn of a phrase. This one, a question, does it for me. Is our church life, is our individual Christian faith, is our collective Christian faith, is our witness and walk with Jesus Christ <u>an upper room foretaste of the eschatology</u>? In other words, do we give off a hint of heaven? Does our life make anyone think of Jesus?

Visiting a little church, I went in to pray. Sitting in a pew I found a piece of paper with this striking verse:

> Jesus said to his disciples: "I have come to set the earth on fire, and how I wish it were already blazing." (Luke 12:49).

The verse is set in a troubling context. Jesus goes on to warn that following his way will not be easy. Instead, it will lead to broken relationships, fractured families, and stark divisions. Anyone who has tried to love as fully, to forgive as completely, to sacrifice as personally, to live as boldly as Jesus demands, knows how hard his way is.

The End

The path to excellence always is. Speak to anyone who has excelled, persevered, recovered, achieved or mastered. The path is hard. But always worth it.

Jesus is saying that in Luke 12:49. He has come to do something earth-shaking, humdrum-shattering, world-changing. Bubbling over with excitement he proclaims, "How I wish it were already blazing!" And he could well add, "I can't wait to see it all in action. Let's get started!"

My study Bible is the New International Version (NIV), and it often includes headings for sections of verses. After Jesus expressed zeal for the fire to get blazing, the next batch of verses is titled "Interpreting the Times." If you jump ahead to Luke 14, the middle section is titled "The Parable of the Great Banquet."

Bringing it all together, Jesus calls us to an on-fire passion equal to his, willing to face the signs of our times faithfully, and do it as an upper room foretaste of the eschatology.

Heaven on earth.

Thy Kingdom come; thy will be done on earth as it is in heaven.

Resurrecto continuo.

Easter always.

My Jesus.